Praise fo

An American Muslim Guide to th

"Sohaib Sultan, one of the first professionally trained Muslim chaplains, had a deep connection with the communities he served and had a profound impact on the development of Islamic pastoral and spiritual care in America. He realized in particular the tremendous responsibility of the preacher in presenting the word of God to the hearts of God's servants. In this book, Chaplain Sohaib relays the prophetic principles of preaching along with his own practical wisdom for sustaining a discipline of preaching based on authentic teachings, personal humility, and an ethic of listening and inclusion. Much gratitude to Martin Nguyen as well, who partnered with Sohaib to complete the book which surely will become a standard for years to come."

INGRID MATTSON, professor of Islamic studies, London and Windsor Community Chair in Islamic Studies, Huron University College at Western University

"*An American Muslim Guide to the Art and Life of Preaching* is both a work of art and the work of a life. Dr. Martin Nguyen starts and ends the book with poignant writing that brings tears to eyes long dried from the grief of loss—the loss of Imam Sohaib, a true guide and gift to the American Muslim community. Imam Sohaib returns to us in this book and is present with the reader on every page. It is a practical work from which preachers—men and women—will find guidance and answers to the questions everyone has but few ask and even fewer answer. It is truly a gift to the community of the faithful, and one that will continue to bless us for decades to come."

TAMARA GRAY, executive director and chief spirituality officer of Rabata

"As a chaplain, imam, public speaker, and someone who has delivered sermons for more than twenty years, I would highly recommend *An American Muslim Guide to the Art and Life of Preaching* to anyone who is looking to learn and improve upon their oratory skills. This is one of the first books written in English that is both insightful and simple to understand, while providing its reader with a much-needed roadmap to navigating every aspect one needs to consider when readying both the content they wish to deliver and themselves personally. It's a testament to Sohaib Sultan's commitment to his faith and tradition, and just one of the many ways he continues to benefit us."

KHALID LATIF, executive director, The Islamic Center at New York University

"Imam Sohaib Sultan's book is a unique testament to who he was as a teacher, preacher, and chaplain. He beautifully embodied those roles with thoughtfulness, compassion, and patience. This book is a wonderful window into the mind and heart of a fully engaged religious leader who showed how to preach and teach with consequence and impact."

OMER BAJWA, director of Muslim life,
Yale University Chaplain's Office

"This book is immensely valuable to Muslims studying in divinity schools, chaplaincy programs, imam training programs, and even those in local Muslim mosques who deliver talks and sermons regularly. A truly transformative work on the theoretical and practical approaches to the art of the sermon in Islam."

KHALIL ABDUR-RASHID, Muslim
chaplain at Harvard University

"This book is an essential resource for every American Muslim religious leader and student of Islamic knowledge. Theoretically deep and filled with practical guidance, the work lays out with great precision the role of the teacher-preacher in twenty-first-century America. Together, Sohaib Sultan and Martin Nguyen offer a window into the tradition, ethics, and artistry of Islamic preaching, a window made all the more compelling by the unique circumstances surrounding the book's genesis. The work is of paramount interest to Islamic seminary students and holds the potential to enrich explorations of homiletics across communities of practice."

CELENE IBRAHIM, author of *Women
and Gender in the Qur'an*

An American Muslim Guide to the Art and Life of Preaching

An American Muslim Guide to the Art and Life of PREACHING

Sohaib Sultan

Revised and Expanded with Martin Nguyen

Fortress Press
Minneapolis

AN AMERICAN MUSLIM GUIDE TO THE ART AND LIFE OF PREACHING

Translations of the Qur'an that appear in the book are the authors' own translations unless otherwise stated.

Cover image: Sohaib Sultan at the Diyanet Center of America in Lanham, Maryland. Photo by Arshe Ahmed. Used by permission.

Cover design: Kristin Miller

Print ISBN: 978-1-5064-8333-7
eBook ISBN: 978-1-5064-8334-4

Contents

Contents

In the name of God, the Merciful, the Compassionate

for our living community of faith and the faithful community yet to come

Foreword

by
Martin Nguyen

On the Nature of This Book

This book is a guide on the art and life of preaching. It was written for the many of you who are holding and beholding it now. It is a gift from its author, Sohaib Sultan, to all of us. It is a labor of love born from the fruits of his faith. Whatever wisdom you might find herein, know that it was given with an earnest desire to draw us closer to our Lord and Sustainer and to uplift our worship before the Divine. While the Friday sermon and its accompanying prayer may, in fact, be only one strand in the rich weave of Muslim devotion, Sohaib recognized the pivotal place that it can hold for the faithful and faith-seeking. As he once wrote, "Prayer goes beyond mere ritual—it becomes the source of internal and external transformation, and the necessary component in living the life of a spiritually vibrant and ethically upright human being."[1] He crafted this work in hopes of refining many of the different but interrelated aspects of this congregational religious experience.

His vision and approach were holistic. This book is as much about the knowledge and care placed behind a sermon as it is about the tone, tenor, and shape of that sermon. It is as much about the character of the person delivering these words as it is about the nature and shape of the words themselves. It is as much about tending to the people of faith that fill the worship space as it is about the aesthetics and arrangement of that same space. This is all to say that this book on preaching is not meant for preachers alone. It was written for us all, whether we are called to address and care for a congregation or we are one of the many called to be part of one.

In fact, it is clear to me that Sohaib drew deeply upon his personal experiences to develop this book: his early years as a maturing, dedicated, and intentional preacher but also a lifetime as an earnest and invested congregant looking to the pulpit for inspiration, guidance, and an example to follow. Having grown up in different parts of the United States and moving between different mosque communities, Sohaib had the opportunity to appreciate the Friday prayer service in all its experiential complexities. He was well aware of how a community might welcome the faithful and faith-seeking but also how easily it could alienate and estrange them as well. As he once said, "And if a space has been carved out for you, then that means you're accepted. It means you're accepted and maybe even celebrated. But if a space has not been carved out for you, it means you're on the periphery. It means you're not even welcome."[2] While many things contributed to these dynamics, Sohaib knew what power and potential a riveting Friday prayer service might hold. At the same time, he had also witnessed its shortcomings: missed opportunities, unnecessary limitations, and the distancing effect a service might yield. This book, then, represents his lifelong commitment to honoring and elevating the experience of the Friday prayer service for his fellow Muslims.

As I hope these pages evince, Sohaib was committed to continually improving the life of faith at both a personal and communal level. This will be no surprise to anyone who knew him. He possessed a great and deep love rooted in faith. For those who heard him speak as a chaplain and preacher, it was clear that he was sensitive to the weight of words and the deliverance or detriment that they might wield. As he once shared, "When we do preach, we have to be very careful about what we say and how we say it, because preaching can sometimes be uplifting and inspiring and encouraging, but it can sometimes really push people away as well."[3] Sohaib chose his words carefully, mindful of the community before him. His words, however, went beyond the immediate message they delivered. They were more dynamic. They were crafted to create and hold space. They were spoken with care and affection. They were meant to uplift the lost and fallen and convey the joys of faith. They were aimed at the softness of our hearts and the reasonable imaginings of our minds. His words here, effused with his characteristic wit and wisdom, are his attempt to translate *his* vibrant life of faith into a guide for us all, especially those beloved communities across North America.

The rendering of these ideas into words and then into the presently printed pages, however, took time, and something must be said of how this book came to be.

On the Making of This Book

This book was long in the making. It was written across the span of life and death. Sohaib and I began our collaboration on this book nearly a year before his passing from this life and this world. While we made significant strides in those twelve months, it became clear during his final weeks that this was an undertaking that I would have to see to completion without him. Then on the evening of April 16, 2021, the first Friday of the blessed month of Ramadan, Sohaib left us for the life to follow. I have spent the months since his death laboring to finish what he had begun long ago. In fact, while I may be writing these words several months after Sohaib's death, he first wrote this book over a decade ago and went on to enact, embody, and refine its principles and teachings in his years of service to many different Muslim communities since its initial composition. Indeed, the life of this work extends at least a dozen years into the past.

Sohaib first wrote this book during his time at Hartford Seminary. He first arrived at Hartford in 2004, where he would pursue a master of arts in Islamic studies and Christian-Muslim relations as well as a graduate certificate in Islamic chaplaincy. This work, however, came some years later and represents his thesis for that program. He submitted it in May of 2010 with the title "Preaching with Purpose: Writing and Delivering Great Sermons." It might seem remarkable for someone to write a book like this while still completing their formation and training, but by this point in his life, Sohaib had already accumulated much experience as a Muslim preacher and chaplain. He had served as the Muslim chaplain at Yale from 2005 to 2006 before moving to Wesleyan University and Trinity College, which he served simultaneously until 2008. By this point, Sohaib had completed his Clinical

Pastoral Education (CPE) and nearly all his coursework. As these experiences came to an end, the work of his thesis still remained. This was a time of transition for Sohaib as well. In 2008, Sohaib left Connecticut for New Jersey to join Princeton University, where he would serve the Muslim community there as its Muslim Life Coordinator for the next thirteen years of his life. It was this position that would prove defining for Sohaib's life, career, and legacy. From it he would build community, forge important ties, and grow personally as a guide and supportive voice for all those who would turn to him for religious guidance and formation.

It was around this time of transition that Sohaib and I would enter the orbit of each other's life. While our acquaintance goes back further, our friendship deepened in 2009, the year I married Kiran Tahir. In fact, it was through her that I got to know Sohaib in a different way because she and Sohaib had been childhood friends. Their families had been part of a close-knit circle of Muslim families in Plainfield, Indiana—that community formed around the Islamic Society of North America (ISNA)—for a span of years important to them both. When Kiran and I moved to Connecticut after our wedding, the opportunities for seeing Sohaib and his wife, Arshe, grew.

During one of our get-togethers, I learned of his thesis and took immediate interest. It struck me as a timely and needed work. Sohaib, of course, also knew this. Having spent his life with different Muslim communities across the United States, Sohaib was keenly aware of how important the sermon could be, but also how variable the quality of its content and delivery. He had already given serious thought to publishing it. After all, this was not Sohaib's first work. He had already published two other books aimed at engaging broader communities: *The Koran for Dummies* (Wiley, 2004) and *The Qur'an and Sayings of the Prophet Muhammad: Selections Annotated and Explained* (SkyLight Illuminations, 2007). Like these earlier publications, his thesis on preaching had intentionally been written to serve as a practical guide. Yet the opportunity, or perhaps urgency, to finally edit and publish the work did not arrive until many years later. It was not until 2020, when the precarity of life became tangible and real, that concrete plans were formed.

In January of that year, two months before the Covid-19 pandemic became a crippling condition for us all, Sohaib and I had the chance of seeing each other one more time. Our families gathered in New Haven at the home of our mutual friends Lisa Kinney-Bajwa and Omer Bajwa, the Director of Muslim Life at Yale and Sohaib's longtime companion through the Hartford Seminary program. The events of that evening were as warm and memorable as any other. But looking back, two moments stand out from that gathering with a bit more weight. First, I made mention of his thesis once more, this time offering my help to edit it. Second, I remember a comment made in passing that ought to have been forgotten otherwise. Sohaib told us of a lingering feeling of unwellness that he could not quite shake. Seemingly a minor matter at the time, the weight of his words would become magnified soon enough. A few months later Sohaib shared with us all that he had been diagnosed with stage-four cholangiocarcinoma, a rare and aggressive form of bile-duct cancer. His case was terminal. Doctors hoped, as they are inclined to do, that he had at most a year or so of life left to him. The ending to Sohaib's life had been written, as it is for us all, but the imminence of his end had become suddenly and sharply more legible for him.

His impending demise was difficult to come to terms with in those early days. Yet being one keen to the measure and power of words, I also thought of the words that Sohaib might leave behind. I thought once more of his thesis on preaching, words he crafted with the intention of one day sharing. So it happened that on April 22, I wrote to Sohaib once more about his book. I asked him if I might help him in seeing it to publication and offered to shoulder the bulk of the work necessary to bring it to press. I made it clear that I was willing to dedicate as much time as needed to revise and expand his thesis into the book he wanted to leave behind. The next day, he texted me with genuine enthusiasm. Although he had spent the past few days hospitalized, he shared with me these words: "I want to do this collaboration and would love to be able to leave something behind for the community on the topic of preaching as a *sadaqa jariyya*."[4] And with that, our work together on this project began.

By May of 2020, I had read through the entire work, and we began to plan out an approach to its revision. We spoke at length about the work that lay ahead of us. The chapters of the thesis, as written, were already well framed and articulated. Minor edits and updates needed to be done. We also agreed, however, on the need to add a new chapter that would somehow incorporate his more than a decade's worth of experience leading and guiding the Princeton Muslim community. Specifically, I suggested that we develop a new chapter that addressed the remarkable measures his community had taken to broaden and elevate the experience of its women members. On the occasions that I had traveled down to Princeton on a Friday, I was struck by the prominent role that the women in his community played in the service. Women recited the Qur'an aloud for the benefit of the congregation. They delivered moving and eloquently crafted supplications after the conclusion of the Friday prayer service itself. They possessed an active and engaged presence with this vibrant Muslim community. It was evident that there was a faith-infused sense of belonging that Sohaib had had some part in fostering and nurturing around the space and time of the Friday prayer. Aware of larger conversations taking place across the Muslim American horizon and mindful of the concerns animating his own congregation, Sohaib recognized the benefit that sharing these experiences might have for Muslim communities farther afield. Nevertheless, he also realized that each congregation was different and warranted careful consideration given the character and circumstances of that community. As he once disclosed, "I go into it with some trepidation . . . because I think a good *khaṭīb* considers their context, and every institution has a context. And so, if I'm at Princeton, Princeton has a context. The university setting has a context, and I can't ignore that by any means. It's different from preaching at a mosque."[5] While Muslim communities across this country might be facing a common set of questions and concerns, it was not a matter of finding a one-size-fits-all solution. The desire to share the experiences born out of his time at Princeton, then, was not envisioned as a prescriptive measure but is offered instead in a spirit of sharing and consultation.

Over the course of the months to follow, we endeavored to call each other at least once every two weeks to continue our work around the project. Unfortunately, we were not always able to connect. There were times when Sohaib was unable to muster the strength in the hour leading up to a call, and we would defer to the next day or following week. Despite the vicissitudes of his health and the other demands of family and community, we kept at the work before us as diligently as we could. There were months animated with excitement and energy. There were months when time slipped away. Yet through it all, we persisted in our collaboration.

By the end of October, I had completed revisions to his original introduction. By November, Sohaib had read through and approved that initial work. In 2021, February saw a flurry of activity. In quick succession, I sent off revisions to chapters 1, 2, and 3. While these numerous edits were being made, Sohaib and I made significant progress on the new chapter as well. Back on November 22, 2020, Sohaib had written the first few pages for it. Therein he described the steps and measures explored by his community and the larger concerns shaping the conversation. Four months later on March 26, 2021, Sohaib drafted a new set of pages to add to the earlier ones. These two sets of pages on women and the Friday prayer service would serve as the basis for the new chapter that I was to compose. The work of synthesizing and expanding upon these pages, however, would have to wait many months more.

While all this work was taking place, Sohaib and I also began to discuss publishers. The work was written for a Muslim audience and centered upon the particularities of the Friday prayer service. Both of us recognized, however, that this work would have broader relevance and could potentially garner interest beyond our immediate community of faith. First, much of the guidance offered by Sohaib in his book, while crafted with the Friday prayer service in mind, was applicable in many contexts beyond it. As Sohaib once shared elsewhere, "If you're not preaching from the pulpit, meaning the *jumuʿa khuṭba*, just the skills of speaking in a way that conveys a message and wisdom to people is important in whatever other setting you might find yourself."[6] Preaching does not happen solely from the pulpit but is needed and undertaken in many places for many people. Sohaib hoped that all those who might find themselves addressing faith-minded audiences might learn something from the advice he had to share. More than that, both Sohaib and I recognized the immense benefit we had gained from engaging with the spiritual and theological works of other faith traditions. In fact, the careful reader will see that Sohaib drew heavily at times from the wisdom and writing found in similarly oriented works written by Christian authors. While certainly drawing on his own experiences and the traditions of Islam, Sohaib also benefited from those works written on the art of preaching (or homiletics, as the discipline is known) in the Christian tradition.

It was in this spirit that Sohaib sought to publish with a press that would make his work accessible to Muslim readers as well as broader readerships. Thanks to a recommendation from a colleague and friend, I reached out to Fortress Press, getting in touch with editor Scott Tunseth. After our initial exchange, I submitted a proposal where I outlined the work already done and the remaining work to do. It was in the midst of these conversations that I went and saw Sohaib in person for the last time. On March 6, 2021, Kiran and I took our daughter down to Princeton to spend time with Sohaib and his family. While we discussed many things, we turned eventually to the work of the book and the prospect of publishing with Fortress Press. It was during this conversation that Sohaib impressed on me his desire to work with Fortress or a press very much like it. Its operation and reach matched well with where Sohaib hoped his book would go. He wanted his work to reach beyond the envisioned Muslim American audience in hopes of nourishing others beyond our immediate concern. Although Sohaib would not be able to see the contracts drawn up before his passing, he was an integral part of those discussions up until his final days.

After that last visit on March 6, Sohaib and I struggled onward with the revisions, although the work became increasingly difficult. On March 28, 2021, Sohaib and I spoke on the phone once more. This time, however, he was not at home but some distance away. He shared with me on that call that he was lying in a hospital bed in Philadelphia gazing up at the towering buildings just outside his window. He was waiting, with his characteristic patience, for a blood transfusion, a necessary but painful procedure. The last transfusion, he shared, had been truly taxing. Unbeknown to me at the time, this was also the last time that we would actually be able to speak to each other, one friend to another. Despite the increasing hardship that the pain of his last days would bring, we continued to exchange messages when possible. Sohaib sent me his final contribution on April 6. It was a document collecting supplicatory prayers from the women of his community. These heartfelt prayers, originally delivered after Friday prayer services, were intended to constitute the appendix that would close the book. In a gesture that so beautifully captures Sohaib's spirit and character, he wanted to share within the space of his work the beauty and faith expressed by others from his community.

Ten days later, Sohaib passed away, and the work of this book passed into a period of quiet grief. Many weeks would pass before I could seriously tend to this work again, but both deadlines and a desire to honor my friend compelled me to pick up the editor's pen once again. I can but pray that I have done this work and its author Sohaib Sultan justice. It is my genuine hope, for those of you who knew him but also for the many others who did not, that you can hear his voice clearly throughout these pages—suffused, of course, with his characteristic wit and wisdom. He wrote very much like he spoke—with thoughtfulness, practicality, and genuine care. I have done my best to refine and preserve his voice and his vision for this book. The space of this foreword and the afterword to come at the end were spaces that we decided were to be reserved for me, the editor of this work and Sohaib's friend and collaborator. While I have arguably taken enough of your time with my words, Sohaib encouraged me to draft what I had envisioned as a "theology of the sermon." Upon further reflection, however, I believe it more appropriate to conclude this foreword and introduce Sohaib's work with what I would call a brief theology of the spoken word.

A Theology of the Spoken Word

The spoken word is a subtle matter. It does not seem to endure in the same manner as the written word. When words are written, they may wait long and patiently before being read and understood. The spoken word, rather, looks as if it lives only in the moment of its delivery—its span extending from the instant it issues into the world to its reception by its hearers. Yet the spoken word is not defined by its utterance alone. There is much more to it than that. It is also shaped by the form of its delivery, the space in which it emerges, and the various ways that it is received, understood, and embodied.

Unfortunately, ours is a time when the spoken word is all too often given little credence or quickly dismissed. Because it is spoken, some imagine it as fleeting and ephemeral. Who has time to pause, listen, and reflect? Who can even hear it through the droning noise of our every day? What chance does the spoken word have in our material world? We lend greater weight, it would seem, to the written word—words committed to ink, words fixed in print, words saved into server-sustained digital clouds.

Yet this disposition fails to appreciate how the spoken word can cut and endure. It can cut through morass to clear a path. It can cut away roughness so that only jeweled facets remain. It can cut deeply down to the marrow so that we never forget. It can cut across time and space to travel beyond the confines of its utterance. Words well spoken, then, may first strike ears in a specific moment but can reverberate long afterward down the corridors of history. Indeed, the spoken word may leave a mark far weightier than those committed to the page. As our lives attest, do we each not have inscribed in our memories words of wisdom spoken by those who came before us? Can we not think back to remarks made by our elders and beloveds—said at just the right time—that remain with us still? And are these same spoken words not passed down by word of mouth to those that come after us? The spoken word, which might seem ephemeral at first, can live long beyond the moment in history in which it is uttered.

I argue that the very life of faith itself finds its shape in words that are spoken. After all, it is through the spoken word that Islam arises and irrupts into the world. The bodies of guidance that constitute the core of this faith—the recited Qur'an and the recollected sayings of the Prophet Muhammad ﷺ—were bestowed upon us through the spoken word. And then, when we have sought to preserve and share these words, are we not keen to maintain that spoken quality that accompanied them? It is not insignificant that God calls the Qur'an *kalām Allāh*, "the Word of God" or "God's Speech" (Q. 2:75; 9:6; 48:15). More than merely an inscribed book bound between two covers, the Qur'an is God's revelation, the disclosure of the Divine to humankind, sent down from on high so that we who live down low might come to know God's will. And is it not the case that the Qur'an is a revelation meant to be recited? Is it not a revelation to be heard? Is it not a revelation to be remembered and recollected? As the twelfth-century theologian Abū Hafs al-Nasafī (d. 537/1142) declares in his doctrinal creed, "The Qur'ān, the Speech of Allah, is uncreated and it is written in our volumes, preserved in our hearts, recited by our tongues, heard by our ears, [yet] is not a thing residing in them."[7] How striking is it, then, to realize that in the Qur'an and through it, God is speaking. How profound is it to know that God speaks and continues to speak to us here and now. This Qur'an, the eternally spoken Word of the Divine, addresses each and every one of us across time and space in a manner that is both intimately personal and bindingly universal. Although the Qur'an descended across the span of twenty-three years, it came to be inscribed into the hearts of the faithful so that it continues to speak to, within, and through its community of hearers.

Of course, the Qur'an is not the only spoken word that reverberates within the tradition of Islam. Consider too the sayings of the Prophet Muhammad ﷺ, the reports of which number in the thousands. The words that he spoke were uttered across so many moments of his life in response to a spectacular array of human experiences and relationships. Despite how these words were embedded in his biography, the faithful since then have diligently sought to keep these words alive in *their* memories and deeds. The words spoken by the Prophet ﷺ, then, can be said to address us and guide us still. These spoken testaments, the Qur'an and sayings of the Prophet ﷺ, deeply inform the religious texts that are penned; they shape the lessons of faith that we impart and imbibe; and they inflect the grammar of our everyday lives. It seems impossible to imagine the Muslim life of faith without the spoken words of God and the Prophet ﷺ to accompany and support us. That a word is spoken makes it no less valuable than a word written.

It should come as no surprise, then, that the spoken word has long maintained an honored place within the devotional lifeways of Muslims. The recitation of the Qur'an continues to fill our lived spaces. Prayers and blessings upon the beloved Prophet ﷺ continue to adorn our gatherings. The aural transmission of the sayings of the Prophet Muhammad ﷺ still holds a valued place in our circles of religious learning. Our poets, performers, storytellers, preachers, and teachers have all made wise use of the spoken word in their respective arts. Indeed, the sermon of the weekly congregational prayer remains a constant reminder of the power that the spoken word can have. Delivered before innumerable congregations across the Muslim world and spanning centuries of Islamic history, the Friday sermon is a constant site where great potential might be brought to fruition. Nevertheless, this potential has not always translated into actuality. Words may well be spoken from a pulpit, but that is no guarantee of quality. All too often, the sermon leaves much to be desired, despite the transformative promise that lies within it. In part, this is why we have invested much of our time into understanding and refining this dimension of our ritual lives. How might our words be spoken in ways that both honor and draw on the distinguished precedents that come before us? How might we render and deliver the spoken word such that it uplifts, challenges, and ennobles?

A dynamic and poignant model emerges from the reports of the Prophet Muhammad ﷺ, specifically from a special class of the spoken word—his sermons. Preserved among the prophetic sayings are the carefully crafted words that the Prophet Muhammad ﷺ delivered in counsel and guidance to his devoted community.[8] Indeed, it is these very sermons that establish the precedence for the congregational prayer service that Muslims worldwide continue to abide by down to this day. While many sermons have come down to us, one sermon arguably stands above the rest in the hearts and memory of the faithful—the farewell sermon, which the Prophet ﷺ reportedly delivered on the ninth of the Islamic month of Dhū'l-Ḥijja in the tenth year after the migration of the Muslim community from Mecca to Medina, or March 6, 632 CE. This sermon, delivered before pilgrims resting outside the vicinities of Mecca, has come to occupy a fixed place in the collective memory of the faithful such that it lives on in the present. The words of the sermon have been preserved in numerous sources, both well-known hadith collections and revered biographies of the Prophet ﷺ. While I will not reproduce it here, in the brief course of the sermon, the Prophet ﷺ addresses a wide array of subjects, including the honoring of the sacred, ritual observance, the care of property, marital relations, and the importance of faith and righteousness over prejudicial notions of hierarchy and supremacy among other matters. This sermon, an exemplar of the spoken word, continues to speak whenever the devout read its words, whenever preachers weave it into their address, or whenever elders draw on its wisdom for the benefit of generations to come.

My main aim, however, is not to analyze the sermon for its message or the manner of its address. I invoke it now, rather, for the parallel that I see. The timing of this sermon is significant in that the Prophet ﷺ would pass from this life only a few months later. For this reason, it earns its name, *khuṭba al-widāʿ*, or the farewell sermon. Though he may not have known the precise moment of his demise, the Prophet Muhammad ﷺ was aware that his passing drew near. He could feel the imminence of the end. As one account relates, he acknowledged this impending reality with his opening words: "Hear me, O people, for I know not if ever I shall meet with you in this place after this year."[9] Furthermore, he offered this farewell address in the midst of teaching his community the rites of the Ḥajj pilgrimage. While gathered in the ʿUrana Valley west of Mount ʿArafa, the Prophet ﷺ was moved to speak these words to his devoted followers as a public farewell. They were spoken to fill the moment but also to outlast it. They were offered so that the wisdom and truth therein might endure well beyond a single lifetime. These were words that the Prophet ﷺ hoped others might live by.

As I pen this meditation in the wake of Sohaib's departure from this life, the opening words to the farewell sermon strike me with added poignancy. Although separated by fourteen centuries, there is a resonance between the farewell sermon and these parting words from Sohaib. The words that the Prophet ﷺ spoke that day in 632 CE were intended to be carried on long after he would leave us. In a similar fashion, the present undertaking—this book—was brought together so that Sohaib's words might be remembered and recalled in the manifold years that still lie ahead. While it is true that this book gathers Sohaib's written words, they were marshaled to honor and uplift the spoken word. With the imminence of his own end poignantly disclosed, Sohaib gathered his words here so that others might turn the spoken word of the sermon into a source of refinement for the faith of others as well as themselves. These are words aimed at upholding the prophetic model of preaching. These are words intent on bringing out the beauty and power that spoken words can possess. These are words that Sohaib has shared in order to remind us that the spoken word is both an art form and a way of faithful living.

Nonetheless, it would be a mistake to rest too much weight upon the sermon alone. While the sermon might well have the potential to do wondrous work with respect to the life of faith, it should not be taken for more than it is. As I have mentioned, what power it might be made to possess is but a shadow of the majesty found in the recited Word of God and an echo of the wisdom of the Prophet Muhammad ﷺ. The sermon in and of itself is not automatically worthy of praise. Rather, its value for the life of faith is measured by its message, its mode of delivery, and the model of living that accompanies it. The scholars of our tradition took the time to address the sermon precisely because sermons can so frequently fall short of our hopes and expectations. Sermons can falter in tone and delivery. They can fall into repetitive and lackluster formalisms. They can be blind to the needs of those they address. They can fail to understand a community's concerns and context. They can be coopted for ideological ends and personal agendas. They can close doors that ought to remain open. They can lead us into greater despondency and decline. Sermons can even fall out of the orbit of their axial inspirations, the sayings of the Prophet ﷺ and the words of the Qur'an. It is precisely because we have experienced sermons that hinder and harm the life of faith that we have turned to preachers like Sohaib to provide us with models and visions for how they ought to be.

We must also keep in mind, moreover, that as central as the recurring sermon may be in the Muslim ordering of life, it also marks only one way for us to devotionally engage with the promise of the spoken word. Indeed, the sermon has no exclusive hold on the spoken word in the life of faith. The Qur'an and sayings of the Prophet ﷺ—as examples of spoken words themselves—should suffice to make this point. Yet it should also be said that each of us can bear and share the spoken word in many other faithful ways. In this light, consider prayer. At its heart, prayer is also a matter of spoken words. These words, however, are not spoken with tongue and mind alone but also enfolded in the bending, bowing, and prostrating of our bodies. It is enunciated with the raising and folding of our arms. It is formed with the movement of many bodies moving in unison, like letters strung into poetic verse. The spoken word, then, need not be delivered from a pulpit nor at the head of a gathering to nourish souls. Nor need it issue in Arabic, but it can go forth garbed in our vernaculars. The faith-filled spoken word may indeed issue from a multitude of places upon manifold tongues. It can be gifted to another when close beside. It can be made to resonate and reverberate when softly given. It can irrupt from below to confront those in power as sharp critique. In fact, the spoken word need not be specifically addressed but can be born aloft to strike what ears it might find. It passes between parents and kin as well as among strangers and friends. It can be somber or joyous, stayed or musical. It can accompany moments both heavy and light. The words we speak in faith can be these many things, for we have felt them—or hoped for them—at different points in our lives. The spoken word, whether as a sermon or in a form otherwise, is efficacious only insomuch as we seek to faithfully transform ourselves as we do others. After all, the quality of the spoken word is inseparable from its source, the heart and character of the speaker.

All of this is to say that great care and reflection ought to accompany the words we speak, and how we speak them. Sohaib knew this well. As he once shared, "It's about education, it's about awareness, it's about learning. But it's really about immersion. You have to immerse yourself into your community and learn and really hear firsthand about the different issues that people face. And through that, gain the sensitivities that are required to be able to offer the right type of preaching."[10] Although Sohaib is no longer with us in this life and this world, he continues to encourage and support us through the words of this book, written for us here so that we might speak more faithfully and righteously.

Acknowledgments

Truly the most noble of you before God are the most reverent of you.
God is All-Knowing, All-Aware.
—Qur'an 49:13

WHILE I HAD BROACHED THE QUESTION several times with Sohaib, we never had the opportunity to discuss the matter of acknowledgments. Having first drafted this book as his thesis, I knew there were many people from that time in his life that Sohaib would have liked to thank as well as innumerable new ones since then that he would have added. My apologies, then, to the many who were important to Sohaib and loved by Sohaib who do not appear here. May God bless you and grant you goodness: *No leaf falls but that He knows it, nor any grain in the dark folds of the earth, nor anything wet or withered but that it is in a clear Book* (Q. 6:59).

Nevertheless, with this brief space afforded to us, allow me to name a few for whom our gratitude is known and clear. Special thanks to Dr. Ingrid Mattson for the mentorship and direction that she provided during the years that culminated in Sohaib's original thesis and for the continuous support that she has provided in the many years since. Our gratitude too to Omer Bajwa, who helped refine the book as a whole and who offered valuable recommendations with respect to chapter 2. Omer, who closely accompanied Sohaib on their mutual journey into chaplaincy and whom we both count as a near and dear friend, was a welcome conversation partner in this collaborative effort to publish Sohaib's book. We are also deeply indebted to Sabrina Mirza, Yusra Syed, and Rachel Harrell-Bilici for the *duʿā's* they graciously contributed at Sohaib's request. These prayers are shared in the appendix at the end of this volume. May their carefully crafted words serve as a model and inspiration for others.

On a personal note, I found the process of revising this work after Sohaib's passing challenging on many levels, both scholarly and personal. In that respect, I must extend my heartfelt thanks to Lisa Kinney-Bajwa, Abdul-Rehman Malik, Fareena Alam, Sumiya Khan, Hanaa Unus, Younus Mirza, Colleen Keyes, and Bilal Ansari for their openness, advice, and friendship as I worked through the manuscript. In fact, Bilal was especially helpful in directing me to Harvey Stark's dissertation on American Muslim chaplaincy, in which Sohaib had been extensively interviewed. When I subsequently reached out to Harvey, he very generously shared his scholarship with me along with his transcripts of the two interviews he conducted with Sohaib. I have drawn on these valuable resources for the foreword of this book. Thank you, Harvey, for your generosity of spirit and assistance in this project. We are also deeply grateful to Fortress Press, especially our editor Scott Tunseth, for all the care, consideration, and support that has been shown to us throughout this difficult process.

The composition of chapter 5, the new chapter to Sohaib's work, was especially difficult as Sohaib passed away before we could work together to shape his initial thoughts into the chapter we wanted. I must admit that this task delayed the completion of this work the most. In the months after his death, I asked for the help of many eyes to ensure that I had captured his voice and mind on this important matter. I am deeply appreciative, then, for the help of Sabrina Mirza, Wasim Shiliwala, Nihal Khan, Celene Ibrahim, and Sohaib's wife, Arshe Ahmed, in that respect. The chapter is better for your insights, though what faults there may be therein are mine alone.

Arshe, of course, has been indispensable throughout the bringing together of this book. She was with us for our discussions of the book, even at its earliest phases when it was still an idea eager to come into being. She was there by Sohaib's side when he first sat to draft its pages as a thesis, and she is here now as we watch this work enter the world. In fact, the last *duʿā'* to close the book is hers. Without question, Arshe was invaluable in ushering this book to its completion. Similarly, I must offer my own love and thanks to my wife, Kiran Tahir, who likewise was with us each step of the way. Throughout the revisionary process (and for all the time that it has demanded), Kiran has been by my side with an understanding and support that was both key and critical. She too read parts of this book as I worked to complete it.

More, however, must be said with respect to family. After all, a work like this, which developed across a lifetime, could not have come to be without the support of those closest to us. Love and gratitude to Sohaib's parents, Talat and Amra Sultan; his sister, Sohaira Sultan; and his nephew, Ayyoob, and niece, Rumaysa, for you were always with Sohaib, in presence or thought, as he undertook the working of these words. With the mention of Ayyoob and Rumaysa, allow me to also name each of our daughters, Radiyya Nusayba Ahmed-Sultan and Maryam Ella Nguyen. This book was brought to be with you and the future generations that you represent in mind. Woven into the fabric of this book is a vision of a coming community of faith for which we have labored and prayed. May you both find yourselves, *insha'Allah*—if God wills—in the company of the righteous and faithful in the years ahead, and may the beauty of the spoken word envelop and accompany you for all the years of your lives. *Amīn.*

Introduction

In the name of Allah, the Benevolent, the Compassionate,
All praise is due to Allah, the Sustainer and Nurturer of the heavens and earth.
Peace and blessings upon the Beloved of God, Muhammad ﷺ
And upon his family, and upon his companions,
And all those who follow him till the Day of Resurrection.

The Muslim Preacher and the Friday Sermon

Every Friday throughout the world, Muslims gather together in villages, towns, and cities to fulfill one of God's commandments: *O you who have faith! When the call to prayer is made on the day of congregation (yawm al-jumuʿa), hasten to the remembrance of Allah and leave off trade* (Q. 62:9). The farmer in Indonesia, the small business owner in Mali, the taxi driver in the busy streets of Egypt, and the corporate banker in Manhattan, all pause for an hour of their day to respond to this call. Listening to the *jumuʿa khuṭba*, or Friday sermon, forms the crux of this religious ceremony. Broadly speaking, the purpose is to celebrate God and to remind the believers of their spiritual and ethical commitments as servants of the Benevolent.

The *khaṭīb*, or Muslim preacher, has a special position and responsibility within a Muslim community to enrich the lives and guide the hearts of a congregation—with God's assistance and permission (*ṭawfīq*). In the words of the famous scholar-preacher Abū al-Faraj Ibn al-Jawzī (d. 597/1201), "[God] has commissioned the vigilant man to arouse those who have fallen into a deep sleep."[1] This tradition of preaching on Friday began with the very advent of Islam—the Prophet Muhammad ﷺ being the first *khaṭīb*—and continues to this day. In fact, the directive to call people to a life of God-consciousness, or *taqwā*, is found in many Qur'anic passages, such as, *And remind, for truly the Reminder benefits the faithful* (Q. 51:55) and *Call to the way of your Lord with wisdom and goodly preaching* (Q. 16:125).

The Messenger of God ﷺ encouraged preachers within his own community to "preach on," as it were:

> Abū Umāma said: "The Messenger of God once performed the prayer while a man from the Anṣār was sitting not too far away narrating stories to the people and admonishing them; the people were facing in [the preacher's] direction. When the man saw the Prophet approaching he stopped his narration and stood up in the midst of the assembly to greet the Prophet. However, the Prophet beckoned to him with his hand to stay where he was, and the Prophet sat down at the edge of the crowd, not having stepped over a single person. Then, when the man had finished his story, he stood up and went over to the Prophet and sat down with him, and the people turned toward the Prophet, he having been behind them. The Prophet then said [to the preacher]: 'Do not rise up from your assembly and bring your storytelling to a halt, for I was commanded to restrain myself [from interrupting] those who call upon their Lord in the early morning and in the evening 'seeking His face.' "[2]

On another occasion, the Prophet ﷺ is reported to have said, "Praise be to God who has appointed from my Community one who reminds them of the 'Days of God.' "[3] The Prophet ﷺ understood the great need for eloquence to accompany the transmission of religious knowledge, employing the talents of such men as Thābit b. Qays, an orator, and the poet Ḥaṣṣān b. Thābit for this important task.[4] In the same way, the Companions of the Prophet and their pious Successors praised the merits of a good preacher. For example, Abū al-Dardā' al-Anṣārī (d. 32/652) said, "A believer can never give alms (*ṣadaqa*) more pleasing to God than an admonition (*maw'iza*) by means of which he exhorts people so that they will be able to leave the meeting having been blessed by God."[5]

The need for effective preachers was considered of primary importance to teach and exhort the masses, especially as Islam spread quickly to many different parts of the world in a short period of time. Historians Jonathan Berkey and Konrad Hirschler document how religious scholars critiqued the authority of the preachers who often drew on nonscholarly sources or lacked a proper religious education.[6] According to Berkey, in cities like Basra, "storytellers and popular preachers became the principal channel of instruction for the common people, for those not engaged in a rigorous course of study of the religious sciences under the supervision of one or more scholars."[7] The preacher, then, was seen as able to convey Qur'anic and prophetic teachings to the masses in an accessible and inspirational way, more so than the erudite scholar-jurist. Affirming this evaluation, Ibn al-Jawzī writes,

> He should by no means look down upon the profession (*amr*) of the preacher (*wāʿiẓ*). When he is fully versed in the various sciences and honest in intention all the people benefit from him. A jurist (*faqīh*), or a traditionist (*muḥaddith*), or a reciter of the Quran (*qāriʾ*) is not capable of bringing to God a hundredth of the people the [preacher] is capable of bringing because this latter delivers his exhortations both to the common people and to the elite, but especially to the common people who scarcely ever meet a jurist (*faqīh*), and so they come to [the preacher] with their questions.[8]

In a similar vein, the scholar al-Subkī noted that many religious scholars did attempt to reach larger audiences but lacked the mobile dynamism of the preacher. As al-Subkī relates, "He is someone who reads to the common people from edifying stories, *ḥadīth* and Koran commentary. He shares [this characteristic] with the preacher (*qāṣṣ*), but they are different in the sense that the preacher recites by heart in the streets, sitting or standing."[9] While some religious scholastics might read to the populace while seated in the mosque, preachers could reach audiences in a variety of other public spaces.

Naturally, Islamic preachers became highly revered and beloved, and sometimes controversial, in Islamic history.[10] Thousands of people would flock to hear famous preachers, and some of those preachers were even more trusted in their opinions than the renowned jurists of their time. Ibn al-Jawzī narrates a story in which the preeminent scholar-jurist Imam Abū Hanīfa's own mother refused to accept one of her son's juristic rulings before confirming it with a revered local preacher in whom she placed enormous trust.[11] As noted by Nehemia Levtzion, "As late as the seventeenth century, according to *Ta'rīkh al-Sūdān*, Sudanese Muslims did not refer to the Cadi [*qāḍī*, or Muslim judge] but preferred to litigate before the preacher, who settled their affair by conciliation."[12] In the books of history, we find wonderful pieces of poetry by the dedicated listeners of preaching describing the greatness of their preacher. For instance, upon delivering a moving sermon, one listener wrote these lines of praise for Ṣāliḥ b. ʿUmar al-Bulqīnī (d. 868/1464): "Our Imam preached [*waʿaẓa*] to mankind—the eloquent man who poured out the sciences like an ocean filled to overflowing and healed hearts with his knowledge and his preaching for only the preaching of a righteous man [*ṣāliḥ*] can heal."[13]

This generally good opinion of, draw to, and need for preaching led to preaching becoming a major religious art in the medieval period.[14] Rhetoric was a required course in Islamic seminaries. Islamic preaching came to be known by different names, each of which conveyed a specific type of preaching within the art. Ibn al-Jawzī identifies three terms that became associated with the art of preaching: *qaṣaṣ* (*qāṣṣ*), *tadhkīr* (*mudhakkir*), and *waʿẓ* (*wāʿiẓ*). He explains what each term means broadly in the art: "The *qāṣṣ* is the one who devotes his attention to stories of the past, narrating them and interpreting them. This is called *qaṣaṣ*. . . . In relating narratives of pious people of old there is a lesson to be gained which gives warning, an admonition which rebukes, and an example of the right to be emulated."[15] Ibn al-Jawzī continues, "As for *tadhkīr*, it consists of informing mankind of the blessing God has bestowed upon them, urging them to render thanks to [H]im and warning them lest they disobey Him. *Waʿẓ*, on the other hand, consists of the instilling of fear that softens the heart."[16] As we will discuss in chapter 3, a good sermon is made of all three characteristics. According to Ibn al-Jawzī, *qāṣṣ* was used to encompass all three genres of preachers.

At the end of the day, however, it was the *khaṭīb*, or Friday preacher, who held the most prestigious position in the preaching class. Aḥmad b. ʿAlī al-Qalqashandī (d. 821/1418), author of a well-known Mamluk guide to administrative responsibilities, claimed that the position of the *khaṭīb* was, "in truth, the most powerful [religious] post and most exalted in rank."[17] The *khaṭīb* not only holds sway over a captive audience that is there to fulfill a religious obligation but also directly emulates the Prophet ﷺ himself—the model *khaṭīb*—in the act of giving the *khuṭba*.[18] Arguably, to this day, the *khaṭīb* is able to influence the community of believers like no one else. For American Muslims, this is particularly true, since the Friday Islamic sermon is for many in the community the only form of religious education and inspiration they have access to on a consistent weekly basis.

However, the unfortunate reality is that the quality of our Friday sermons is often lacking in many aspects and therefore fails to meet the needs of the congregation. Wael Alkhairo, author of *Speaking for Change: A Guide to Making Effective Friday Sermons*, offers this critique on the state of our Friday Islamic sermons: "Today and in the recent past, the Friday speakers (*khaṭībs*) have neglected, for the most part, to raise the intellectual level and sense of responsibility of the Muslims to meet the challenges of our time."[19] Anecdotally, I have had many conversations with Muslims about the dire state of our sermons and the need to raise their quality. The general criticism of the community has largely focused on five core areas:

1. Irrelevance of the content of the sermon to the daily struggles that Muslims face in maintaining and enhancing their faith in the secular modern world
2. Impractical or extreme advice imparted by the *khaṭīb*, who is sometimes removed from or new to the realities of life in the United States
3. Language employed by the *khaṭīb* that is divisive, unnecessarily insensitive, or outright offensive
4. Disorganization of the *khuṭba* so as to make many points without a central focus or message
5. The style, gestures, and demeanor of a *khaṭīb* that can distract and detract from a sermon's content

Now, this is not to criticize all preachers. Many do an excellent job with minimal resources. The burden of responsibility to raise the standards of Friday sermons lies not only with the *khaṭīb* but with the *masjid* (mosque), its institutional management, and the community as a whole. Typical American *khaṭībs* face many challenges that affect the preparation and delivery of their *khuṭbas*. First, the people charged with giving the *khuṭbas*—whether they are official Imams or simple lay preachers—are usually the same people who are expected to fulfill a host of other religious duties for the community while also contributing to the support of their families. As such, these preachers have little to no time for careful and thoughtful *khuṭba* preparation. A second major factor is the lack of training and resources available to American Muslim preachers. Christian preachers, for instance, are expected to receive training at a seminary on the art of preaching. This training is usually fully paid for by the church and is even expected of lay preachers who preach only once in a while. Muslim preachers, on the other hand, have no such training available to them. Similarly, Christian preachers can rely on a whole host of well-written and well-researched books—both traditional and modern—to assist and guide them. Most books available to Muslims on the art of preaching are largely inaccessible and underused medieval texts that need major revisions and updating to be relevant for modern Muslim preachers. A great degree of translation with respect to culture and context is also required for those works already translated into English.

Therefore, this guide is born not only out of a response to the state of our Friday sermons but also out of a desire to encourage and fortify our Islamic preachers—current and future—with a relevant and useful manual on the art of Islamic preaching in twenty-first-century America. While the focus and perspective of this guide is the Friday sermon or *jumuʿa khuṭba*, it is hoped that Muslim preachers in various other settings will also find it to be valuable and pertinent.

The Layout of the Book

This book is divided into five chapters. In chapter 1, I cover the theory of Islamic preaching by looking at both classical and modern works. I also reflect on what Islamic preaching means and demands of us in America today. Chapter 2 will turn from the art of preaching and venture into the life of a preacher with the understanding that the sermon is never divorced from the one charged to deliver its message. Four critical aspects of the life of a preacher are examined: the spiritual, intellectual, physical, and social. Chapter 3 then proceeds to explore the process of how a sermon is conceived, researched, and prepared. This chapter looks at models or patterns that preachers can employ in their sermons, discussing the advantages and disadvantages of each method along the way. I also examine rhetorical devices available to the preacher as they prepare a sermon aimed at capturing people's attention. Moreover, I discuss the importance of knowing one's community of listeners and how preachers can gain access to such knowledge.

Chapter 4 focuses on the delivery of a good sermon. This chapter offers practical advice on how to capture the imagination of a congregation with style and gestures so that a well-written sermon can be turned into a well-preached one. I also explore some of the challenges American Islamic preachers face in preparing and delivering effective sermons—such as diversity and congregational sensitivities—and possible ways of dealing with those predicaments in a healthy and productive manner. This chapter also discusses an effective evaluation process to determine the quality of a sermon by looking at various models for collecting useful evaluations—formal and informal—and the important questions that need to be asked in the process. Lastly, I focus on *khuṭba* ethics that propose a general code of conduct that preachers should try to live up to and that the community should expect.

Given the critical questions being raised in American Muslim congregations on the role and place of women within Muslim religious spaces, chapter 5 explores ways that a community can be more inclusive for both its women and men. I share the story of how such concerns were raised within the Muslim community at Princeton University and then share some of the practices we explored and implemented that benefited the community as a whole. It is my hope that the content of chapter 5 will benefit preachers and congregations facing similar questions and struggles. Then I recommend in the conclusion ways to further develop the art of preaching for Muslims in America. This closing section presents an ambitious but realistic set of initiatives to raise the standards of Friday Islamic sermons, such as developing classes or workshops on *khaṭīb* training; creating a professionally run online platform where Muslim preachers can network, learn, and exchange ideas; and proposing further areas of research to revive the art of Islamic preaching for our times.

The Foundational Sources of the Book

The guidance developed within this work draws on six major sources:

1. *The Qur'an.* Several years ago, I guest lectured at a Princeton Theological Seminary class on the Qur'an. As I began my lecture, I asked students what their initial reflections were upon reading selected sections of the scripture. One insightful student remarked that the Qur'an read like a series of sermons instead of linear stories. The Qur'an,

indeed, is the greatest reminder for the believer! As such, wherever and whenever possible, this guide will support its recommendations with principles and proofs found in God's final revelation. The work not only cites and explains Qur'anic passages relevant to preaching but also offers an analysis on the way in which the Qur'an conveys its message and holds its reader's attention.

2. *Hadith Literature.* The Prophet Muhammad ﷺ was commissioned by God to teach, remind, and warn humanity. There is something to learn from every aspect of the Prophet's life—from his excellent conduct to his beautiful speech—including the content and delivery of his own sermons. As with the Qur'an, I draw on the sayings of the Prophet ﷺ whenever and wherever appropriate.
3. *Classical Islamic Texts on the Art of Preaching.* Of this literature, I pay particular attention to Ibn al-Jawzī's preaching manual, *Kitāb al-Quṣṣāṣ wa'l-Mudhakkirīn* ("The Book of Storytellers and Reminders"). According to Swartz and other scholars, it is among the more mature works on the Islamic art of preaching in that it places the art "on a firmer moral and intellectual foundation."[20]
4. *Modern Muslim Guides on the Art of Preaching.* While rare, several modern compositions and research papers have been written on the topic of preaching. Among them is "The Muslim Friday Khutba: Veiled and Unveiled Themes," an insightful and useful policy paper from 2009 written by Mazen Hashem and produced by the Institute for Social Policy and Understanding (ISPU).[21] Other works of note include Wael Alkhairo's *Speaking for Change: A Guide to Making Effective Friday Sermons* published in 1998, Ibrahim Madani's *The Essentials of Jumu'a* published in 2010, and the concise 2012 guide prepared by Amjad M. Tarsin entitled "A Practical Guide to Giving Friday Sermons" that was made available online.
5. *Christian Works on Homiletics.* This work also draws richly from the books and articles on preaching from the Christian tradition. Christians have a long history of scholarship in this area. Seminary libraries are filled with shelves on the topic. While most of these works are Christian-centric in their approach, they contain nonetheless jewels of wisdom that are universally applicable. My drawing on this body of work is based on the Prophetic counsel: "Any word of wisdom is the

lost possession of the believer, who has the better right to it wherever it may be found."[22] We can also take inspiration from the fact that there is a long tradition of shared learning among the three Abrahamic faiths in particular. Christians, likewise, have benefited much from the gems of Islamic thought over the centuries.

6. *Vocational Experience.* Lastly, this guide draws on my own experiences—both successes and failures—as a *khaṭīb* for more than a decade in various capacities and settings. I offer my own experiences with sincere humility knowing that many others, including some who will read this manual, have had many more years of worthy experience than me. Since the content of this manual is original in some ways, I rely on my own experiences to navigate the difficult terrain of Islamic preaching in America. As I recommend at the end of this book, a future work needs to be written that gathers together the practical wisdom of our best preachers.

Finally, it is important for the author of this book to emphasize that this is an attempt to give long-overdue attention to the art of Islamic preaching. I do not expect or hope this to be the final say on how American Muslim preachers ought to preach. It is my sincere hope that this work will produce the enthusiasm needed to spur more conversation, thought, and research on this critically important subject.

Truly success comes only through Allah—
the Guider of hearts, the Nurturer of noble character,
and the Granter of the gift of speech.

1 On the Purposes of Preaching

SPEECH ALLOWS HUMAN BEINGS TO COMMUNICATE with one another in the most sophisticated, complex, and intelligible of ways. Indeed, the ability to articulate our ideas and experiences is nothing other than a divine gift of the highest magnitude. As God, exalted is He, says in *sūrat al-Raḥmān*, *The Merciful One, who taught the Qur'an, created the human being, and taught them intelligent speech* (Q. 55:1–4). Ronald J. Allen, a leading contemporary scholar of preaching in the Christian tradition, writes,

> Language shapes the ways we think, feel, and act in the world. From the basic "master story" of a culture or community to the tiniest metaphor, our language results in social attitudes, behavior, roles, and structures. Indeed, to use language is to create, or recreate, a world.[1]

This description of the power of words reflects an analogy that Allah the Beautiful has given in *sūrat Ibrāhīm*: *A goodly word is like a good tree, whose roots are firmly fixed, and whose branches reach to the heaven. It brings forth its fruit at all times, by the permission of its Sustainer* (Q. 14:24–25). All of this is to say that the art of preaching—which primarily uses language to move the hearts and minds of people—is a powerful tool that has shaped and continues to shape human civilization. As such, it is imperative for a serious preacher to consider well, from the very onset of their vocation, what the roles and purposes (*maqāṣid*) of preaching are. Before delving into *how* we preach well, we first need to ask ourselves *why* we even preach in the first place. Discovering the purposes of preaching is the first step in nurturing good sermons.

A second but interconnected task is for the American *khaṭīb*, or preacher, to ponder what Islamic preaching in twenty-first-century America means and entails, particularly on the high occasion of the *jumu'a khuṭba*, the Friday prayer service. In his policy paper, Mazen Hashem offers an accurate description of the importance of Friday sermons in today's world, especially here in the United States:

> *Khutbas* may have an importance above and beyond their constituency. Given the absence of a formal religious institutional authority within Islam [especially American Islam], less formal facets assume considerable significance. The *khutbas* are neither irrelevant to the wider Muslim community nor represent its official statements; rather, they contribute to the construction of sites of deliberation. Indeed, a form of public deliberation takes place in social gatherings as the attendees, both those who are impressed and those who are disappointed reflect upon the message. Furthermore, with the expansion of global media, *khutbas* beyond the national boundaries are now available and reaching a new segment of virtual attendees (mostly women).[2]

Given this reality that Hashem describes, it is important for us to reflect on the ways in which our approach to preaching might be different in this age of social deliberation and modern technology.

Upon examining the Qur'an, prophetic traditions, classical sources, and more contemporary interpretations, some core ideas on the purposes of Islamic preaching begin to emerge. I distill these ideas as follows.

Spiritual-Preaching: Inspiring Awe of God, Love for Good Works, and Attention to the Hereafter

Allah the Glorious asks rhetorically in *sūrat fuṣṣilat*, *And who is better in speech than the one who calls to God* (Q. 41:33). This passage indicates that the highest form of speech—and thus preaching—is exhorting people to focus their attention on Allah in the midst of distractions and encouraging them to journey on the road that leads to Allah. The verse, however, does not end there. It goes on to say, *And does righteousness, and says, "Truly I am of those who have willingly surrendered to God"* (Q. 41:33). The idea of preaching closeness to Allah, then, is closely attached to showing people, through deeds and words, how to live a life of goodness by preferring God's teachings and commandments (*islām*) over the carnal desires of the inner appetites, or *shahawāt* (Q. 3:14; 4:27; 19:59), and outer attractions of the life of this world, or *zīnat al-ḥayāt al-dunyā* (Q. 18:28; 18:46). In the very command to gather for Friday prayers, Allah the Sublime states the gathering's purpose as the *remembrance of God* (Q. 62:9). Therefore, the first purpose of preaching is to wake people up from a state of spiritual heedlessness (*ghafla*) to a state of spiritual awareness (*taqwā*). This kind of preaching can be referred to as *spiritual-preaching.*

The method of engendering nearness to Allah involves reminding people of what their natural senses (*fitra*) already know to be true and naturally incline to (*Remind, for truly the reminder benefits the believers* [Q. 51:55])—giving glad tidings (*bashīr*) about the earthly and heavenly fruits of faith, and warning (*nadhīr*) against the consequences of negligent disobedience (*Truly We have sent you [O Prophet] with the truth as a bearer of glad tidings and a warner* [Q. 35:24]). Calling people to Allah also necessarily involves calling people to the way of the Messenger ﷺ, the model for living a life of God-consciousness: *Surely, in the Messenger of God you have a beautiful and excellent example for everyone who longs for God* (Q. 33:21). The entirety of a spiritual-preaching sermon can be dedicated to aspects of the Prophet's life and noble character.

Many of the Prophet's own sermons that are recorded in books of hadith focus entirely on urging the community of believers to turn to Allah by engaging in good works during this short earthly life. One of the Prophet's most repeated sermons was simply a recitation of *sūrat al-Qāf* (Q. 50), which offers powerfully clear arguments for resurrection after death, gives a detailed articulation on the illusions of temporary life and the realities of the eternal afterlife, and reveals the result of living a life of arrogant disbelief versus a life of humble faith. Another example of this type of prophetic preaching is the following short sermon delivered by the Prophet ﷺ:

> Adorn yourselves with obedience [to Allah], and clothe yourselves with awe [of Allah]. And make your Hereafter for yourselves, and strive for your final abode. Know that very soon you will depart [from this world] and your destination is with Allah. Nothing will help you there except a good deed which you have sent forward, or a good reward which you already acquired. Indeed, you will arrive at what you sent forward, and

> you will be rewarded according to what you did. Therefore, do not let the lowly adornments of this world deprive you from the high ranks of paradise. Sooner than you expect, the veil of uncertainty will be removed and each person will discover his final abode.[3]

Classical theories on the purposes of preaching focus almost exclusively on returning people's attention to God (*tawba*), good works, and the afterlife. For example, Imam Abū Ḥāmid al-Ghazālī (d. 505/1111) writes the following in his famous letter to a student, *Ayyuhā'l-walad* ("O My Beloved Son"):

> The idea of admonition is for the worshipper to recollect the fire of the hereafter and his own remissness in the service of the Creator, to consider his past life which he has spent in what did not concern him, and consider what difficulties lie before him such as the absence of firmness of faith in his life's final moments, the nature of his state in the clasps of the Angel of Death, and whether he will be capable of answering Munkar and Nakīr, that he worry about his state during the Resurrection and its episodes, and whether he will cross the Bride safely or tumble into the abyss. The recollection of these things should remain in his heart and upset his apathy. To foment these fires and lament these calamities is termed "admonition" [*tadhkīr*].
>
> Informing mankind and apprising them of these things, warning them of their remissness and negligence, making them see the defects of their egos, so that the heat of these fires impinges on the congregation, and the calamities disturb them so that they make amends for their past lives as far as possible, and they are distressed by the days passed in disobedience to God the Exalted: all of this in this way is termed "preaching" [*waʿẓ*].[4]

Ibn al-Jawzī offers a similar approach to preaching in *Kitāb al-Quṣṣāṣ wa'l-Mudhakkirīn*. He describes preachers as "reformers," "teachers," and "warners" whose task it is to turn people away from "corroding pleasures and frivolous preoccupations."[5] Ibn al-Jawzī goes on to say that preachers are like dams, which regulate a body of water so that the water flows properly and is beneficial rather than destructive to the earth. Likewise, a preacher is tasked with exhorting people to control their passions in ways that benefit rather than harm their souls.[6] Later in the same text, Ibn al-Jawzī commends himself—as a way of legitimizing his theories on the art of preaching—for "exhorting the people and urging them to repent and live lives of righteousness" so much so that "one hundred thousand men repented in [his] presence" and "ten thousand" youth reformed their ways and over "one hundred thousand" converted to Islam.[7] In this description of his preaching efforts, Ibn al-Jawzī conveys what he believes the primary purpose of Islamic preaching to be: calling on people to repent, reform, and revert.

Interestingly, according to Hashem, the most common themes in American Friday sermons reflect this spiritual-preaching approach, in which the primary purpose is to remind and urge the community to prioritize God in their lives, to be diligent in performing good works, and to shun the lower appetites of desires and distractions. Hashem reasons that the impulse for this approach to Friday sermons is found in Islamic spiritual teachings that lean toward the idea that human beings are weak, forgetful, and attracted to sin while also capable of spiritual excellence and moral goodness through consistent reminders of divine teachings.

My own sense is that spiritual-preaching has to be at the heart of Islamic preaching in America today. Many of the social and moral ills of American society, which Muslims are very much a part of, are rooted in negligence of and apathy toward foundational spiritual teachings. Furthermore, the vast number of people suffering from depression and confusion in society is truly troubling. All of this is to say that preaching devoid of a spiritual message is essentially devoid of meaning and relevance. However, if this is the only approach to preaching week after week, this can also be a problem because spiritual-preaching assumes everyone in the congregation is already convinced of Islam's core truths and teachings and that encouraging and reminding them of these principles is the only task at hand. The reality of the situation is that we live in an age of skepticism and relativism in which we are expected to question and doubt everything, including our central beliefs and core values. Furthermore, American Muslims live in a religiously diverse society in which many religious beliefs and practices invite questions from fellow friends, neighbors, coworkers, and classmates. As such, it is as important for the American *khaṭīb* to educate and inform as it is to inspire and exhort.

Teaching-Preaching: Teaching and Guiding People to the Way of Islam

While the first purpose of preaching is to inspire and remind people of God and living a God-conscious life, the interrelated purpose that we examine in this section is teaching people about the inward and outward aspects of the religion and guiding them to the way of truth. The proof of this approach to preaching is in Allah the Magnificent's saying, *Only those of His servants endowed with knowledge are in awe of God* (Q. 35:28). Thus, in order to achieve the first purpose of preaching—engendering nearness to Allah—the supplementary purpose of transmitting proper knowledge about the religious path is needed. In another passage, Allah the Exalted describes His Prophet ﷺ as one who *teaches you the Scripture and wisdom and teaches you that which you knew not* (Q. 2:151). As preachers inheriting the pulpit of the Prophet ﷺ, this important task extends to us in some capacity. Similarly, the Prophet ﷺ advised Ali, may Allah be pleased with him, to strive in guiding people.[8] The Prophet ﷺ is also reported to have said, "If anyone calls others to follow right guidance, his reward will be equivalent to those who follow him without their reward being diminished in any respect on that account."[9] As such, imparting knowledge and guidance to inform a congregation's theological worldview or ethical behavior is an essential function of preaching. This type of preaching can be referred to as *teaching-preaching.*

In one of his sermons, the Messenger ﷺ explains to us the beautiful objectives in spreading knowledge:

> Teach knowledge [of the religion]. To teach it for the sake of Allah is awe of Allah; to seek it is worship; to speak of it is glorification [of Allah]; to study therein is striving; to teach it to someone who does not know it is charity; and to spend on those who possess it is a pious deed. Knowledge clarifies the permissible and the prohibited. It is a lighthouse on the path of travelers to the Garden; it is a friend in the wilderness, a companion in a foreign place, a voice in solitude, a guide in prosperity and in adversity, a weapon against enemies, and an ornament while among friends. Allah uplifts a people through knowledge, making them leaders in goodness, preserving their footsteps and making others follow their actions, considering their opinion as authoritative. The angels are inclined to their friendship and stroke them with their wings. Everything fresh or dry, the fish and

> the creatures of the sea, the wild beasts and the cattle of the land, ask for forgiveness for them. Indeed, knowledge is the life of hearts against ignorance, and the light of eyes against darkness. [Through it], a person reaches the rank of the elíte and high stations both in this world and the next. Contemplation of it is equivalent to fasting and teaching it is equivalent to standing in prayer. Through knowledge one joins the ties of relationship and distinguishes the permissible from the prohibited. [Such] knowledge is the guide to action, and deeds follow it. The blessed are those who are inspired by it, and the wretched are those who are deprived of it.[10]

In this tradition, we find several objectives in spreading knowledge and guidance through preaching: (1) to make clear for people what is right and what is wrong, (2) to serve as a source of illumination in the affairs of a believer in all times and situations, (3) to remove ignorance and enmity from people's hearts, and (4) to guide people to the path of a good afterlife. The Prophet's well-known and fondly transmitted farewell sermon at the Great Pilgrimage (*ḥajj*), *khuṭba al-widāʿ*, is an ideal example of a teaching-preaching sermon in which the sacredness of God, religion, life, human relationships, dignity, and justice were all clearly articulated and explained.

Once again, it is apparent that al-Ghazālī and Ibn al-Jawzī appreciated this idea of spreading knowledge in their own articulations on the purpose of preaching. Al-Ghazālī sees the explicit objective of teaching-preaching as reforming the behavior of individuals:

> Your zealous intention must be to lead men from the world to the hereafter, from recalcitrance to obedience, from acquisitiveness to renunciation, from stinginess to generosity, from doubt to certainty, from indifference to vigilance, and from illusion to God-consciousness. You should evoke in them love of the afterlife and loathing for the world. You should *teach* them about worship and asceticism. . . .
>
> Perhaps their inward qualities will be transformed, and their outward behavior exchanged—"acquisitiveness" and an "appetite" for obedience, and for repentance from disobedience, will appear.[11]

Similarly, Ibn al-Jawzī likens a preacher to an instructor who is responsible for "educating," "reforming," and "nurturing" the masses.[12] Interestingly, Ibn al-Jawzī adds the extra ingredient of "nurturing" as part of the teaching-preaching objective, which indicates that there is also something of a counseling-preaching approach to the overall purpose of preaching—the theme of the next section. Other classical scholars also saw the role of preaching as teaching, such as 'Alī b. Muḥammad b. Wafā' (d. 807/1404), who defined the purpose of preaching as "gathering people together with one who *instructs* them in what is good."[13]

Enthusiastic support for preaching as a tool for education is also found among the thinkers and scholars of twentieth-century Islamic movements. For example, *Let Us Be Muslims* is a well-known English translation of a series of famous Urdu sermons delivered by the late Mawlana Sayyid Abul A'la Mawdudi (1903–79) from the Indian subcontinent. In this book, Mawdudi's sermons are aimed at reviving people's understandings of core concepts in the religion, primarily by answering the questions of *why* rather than the questions of *what.* The purpose of these sermons, then, is to teach and engage the minds of people first and foremost. They are more informative than inspirational.

Echoing this line of thinking, Alkhairo identifies teaching-preaching as the primary purpose of a *jumu'a khuṭba*. After lamenting on the state of the Muslim *umma*, Alkhairo offers the following analysis:

> At the heart of the problem is an ineffective Islamic education methodology. Nevertheless, the *khuṭbah* on Friday, being the most accessible means of educating and revitalizing Islamic thought, can significantly contribute to a solution. . . . The *Jumu'ah's* potential to serve as a "school" that can raise the awareness of the Muslims, appraise them of their worth, individually and as an ummah, inform them of their human rights, responsibility, and mission remains high. . . . [Thus,] the weekly *Jumu'ah* gathering is a school that teaches the ummah.[14]

Here we see, probably for the first time in our discourse thus far, the idea of connecting the individual Muslim to the larger *umma*, another common characteristic of Islamic movement–oriented ideas on the purpose of preaching and one that we will return to in the last section of this chapter. For now, it can be stated that *social-preaching* is similar to the idea of "act locally, think globally" or, in our terms, "preach locally, think globally." Certainly, teaching-preaching and social-preaching naturally go arm in arm (and I discuss social-teaching at length below).

My own sense is that teaching-preaching is a very important purpose of preaching in America today. There are many burning questions and concerns in the hearts and minds of American Muslims that can be addressed through this theory of preaching. However, the key is for preachers to know and identify what these questions and concerns are so that teaching-preaching sermons are relevant and practical for the community of listeners. Interestingly, Hashem notes in his research that the only time preachers would go beyond reminding to actually teaching was when they wanted to clarify some rather minute or controversial theological issue. In my experience, certain preachers are obsessed with these rather menial issues and preach on them frequently. But the community, for the most part, finds little relevance in these issues and has much more serious and greater concerns regarding how to live as good Muslims in America. So for teaching-preaching to work, the American *khaṭīb* has to be in touch with the realities on the ground and ought to preach from that ground.

A second point that I would make is that the American *khaṭīb* must be aware of the fact that he is speaking to, for the most part, a very literate and educated audience. Research studies have shown that the American Muslim community has a high level of academic achievement. As such, teaching-preaching sermons must be prepared in an organized and sophisticated way with arguments that make sense. A teaching-preaching *khuṭba* that does not do this can be counterproductive no matter how good the intention. For example, once I heard a *khuṭba* that attempted to tackle the difficult theological questions that arise out of the scientific theory of evolution. The *khaṭīb* was so ill informed about the science itself that his theological arguments fell flat as a result. The more scientifically informed members of the congregation left the *khuṭba* more dissatisfied than before they entered. On the other hand, I have witnessed several good sermons teaching the community and raising awareness therein about important issues, such as the great evils of domestic abuse. So teaching-preaching sermons are useful and relevant, but they need to be developed carefully and wisely.

Counseling-Preaching: Healing Hearts and Giving Sincere Advice

There are times when preachers find themselves in the position of a community counselor amid chaos, discord, tragedy, or the like that has affected everyone in the congregation either directly or indirectly. In such cases, the preacher is expected to be not only a teacher-preacher but also a sympathetic and compassionate counselor-preacher. While the sermon may include teaching moments, the overall objective and tone of such a sermon is to heal human hearts or offer nurturing advice. This theory of preaching draws its inspiration from two foundational hadiths of the Messenger ﷺ, wherein he says, "The religion is good counsel and goodwill (*al-dīn al-naṣīḥa*)"[15] and "None of you can truly be said to believe until he wants for his brother what he wants for himself (*la yu'minu aḥadukum ḥattā yuḥibba li-akhīhi mā yuḥibbu li-nafsihi*)."[16] This type of preaching can be called *counseling-preaching.*

There are several prophetic narrations that encourage offering relief to fellow Muslims. For instance, the Prophet ﷺ said, "He who removes from a believer one of his difficulties of this world, Allah will remove one of his troubles on the Day of Resurrection; and he who finds relief for a hard-pressed person, Allah will make things easy for him on the Day of Resurrection."[17] Words have an enormous power to relieve psychological and spiritual pain. And this applies all the more to a preacher's sermon, which can offer much healing to a community that is in pain. For example, when I was in college, our Muslim community on campus was struck with the sudden and tragic death of a member of our community. Everyone was in such shock and sadness over the loss. That Friday, the *khaṭīb* gave a moving *khuṭba* on the virtues of making *du'ā'* (supplicatory prayer) for a loved one who has passed away. There was not a single person left in the congregation who was not wiping away tears and with them some of the pain of the loss. This was counseling-preaching at its best. At other times, there are larger world events that cause sadness or distress, such as major natural disasters or wars, that call for the preacher to preach as a counselor.

Frequently, the objective of preaching is to address major religious questions or concerns that a community or segment of the community may have. Addressing these questions can take on a teaching-preaching purpose, but sometimes a counseling-preaching perspective might be more useful when the issue at hand does not have an easy answer or when the issue is tangled with emotional knots. For instance, I was called upon once to preach at a Muslim-run shelter for abused women. Many of these women were seriously considering leaving their husbands, but they were afraid for their personal safety or the loss of their children. In such a situation, a counseling-preaching sermon that focused on how to make decisions and rely on Allah in our personal affairs made more sense than a teaching-preaching sermon on the *fiqh* of divorce or the like. Another good example is a *khuṭba* that offers advice on how to raise spiritual and ethical children today. The purpose of such preaching is to offer the best and most sincere counsel possible to a congregation that may be dealing with similar problems.

Social-Preaching: Calling to Social Goodness, Peace, and Justice

The last broad purpose of Islamic preaching is to inspire—using the method of reminding, teaching, and counseling—the local and global *umma* so that together, Muslims are called upon to live the teachings of their faith. Allah the Just says in *sūrat āl ʿImrān*, *Let there arise out of you a group of people inviting to all that is good, enjoining what is right and forbidding what is wrong* (Q. 3:104). The preachers of Islam must be among this group of people, and one of the primary purposes of preaching must be to pursue this Qur'anic injunction of enjoining social goodness. Likewise, Allah the Wise encourages peacemaking at a time of local or global conflict in several passages, including *sūrat al-ḥujurāt*: *The believers are but brethren, so make peace between your brethren and keep conscious of God so that you might be graced with mercy* (Q. 49:10). Of course, peacemaking must first begin at home within the congregation of the preacher. Similarly, the Prophet ﷺ said, "Whoever amongst you sees an evil he must change it with his hand, if he is not able to do so then with his tongue," and "The most excellent sacred struggle (*jihād*) is speaking the truth in the presence of a tyrannical ruler."[18] So the preacher is granted the pulpit by the permission of God, in part, to pursue justice by either encouraging it or discouraging its opposite. All of this can be called *social-preaching*.

An excellent example of this type of preaching is in a sermon delivered by the Messenger ﷺ on the rights that fellow believers have upon one another:

> Avoid suspicion, for indeed suspicion is the greatest falsity in speech. Do not spy, do not seek out information [about others], do not fight, do not envy, do not harbor malice, and do not despise one another, but be servants of Allah as brothers, as Allah Most High has commanded you. The Muslim is a brother to a Muslim. He does not treat him unjustly, forsake him or look down on him. It is a sufficient evil for a person to look down on a brother Muslim. Everything belonging to a Muslim is sacred to another Muslim: his property, his blood, and his honor. Indeed, Allah

> does not look at your faces and your forms, but He looks at your hearts and your deeds. Piety is here, piety is here, piety is here . . . [pointing to his blessed heart] Do not bid against one another but become servants of Allah as brothers. It is not permissible for a Muslim to be estranged from his brother for more than three days.[19]

This purpose of preaching seems to be largely missing from classical sources, but it is quite dominant in more contemporary Muslim preaching. In Alkhairo's guide to preaching, he writes,

> The weekly Friday sermon, the *khutbah*, and the Friday prayer (*salat al Jumu'ah*) are powerful institutions that were established to build communities. They provide an opportunity for spiritual nourishment, learning, and group bonding. By serving as a constant reminder of the individual's relationship with Allah and his belonging to the community of believers (*ummat al Islam*), the *khutbah* infuses the Muslim character with the mission of vicegerency (*khilāfah*) on the Earth, both individually and as a community (*ummah*). Utilized properly, it can be an effective means of producing long-lasting positive changes—spiritual, ethical, and cultural—within the community identity.[20]

My own sense is that the American Muslim community is still very much in its formative period, and its communal identity is constantly being shaped every day by various forces. As such, the American *khaṭīb* has a responsibility to enter this communal shaping process headlong to ensure that its development is sound and wholesome. The American Muslim community is still also trying to find its place in the larger American society and is struggling to find a role for itself. Preaching is an effective tool to push the community toward a sense of purpose that is rooted in goodness, peacemaking, and social justice. Of course, this type of preaching has its drawbacks when preachers preach passionately rather than responsibly and when sermons become rants rather than well-thought-out visions. Moreover, social-preaching must always be tempered by spiritual-preaching because the root problems of social issues always go back to the spiritual defects in the hearts of people.

In conclusion, the author of this preaching manual trusts that the four abovementioned purposes or modes of preaching are broad enough to encompass more minor purposes. These four modes should not be understood as isolated approaches but be joined dynamically together into the art of Islamic preaching. Any one sermon can contain one or more of these purposes in its objective and content. It goes without saying that the purposes of Islamic preaching can only be met by effective preaching. Much of the remainder of this preaching manual focuses on just that. For now, let us conclude with this beautiful verse from *sūrat al-nahl* as food for thought as we move on to the next chapters: *Call unto your Sustainer's path with wisdom and beautiful exhortation, and discourse with [people] in the kindest manner* (Q. 16:125).

2 On the Life and Character of a Preacher

Allah the Sublime warns believers against hypocrisy in several passages that are particularly relevant to the Islamic preacher. In *sūrat al-baqara*, God asks, *Do you enjoin people to piety, while you forget your selves?* (Q. 2:44). Then in *sūrat al-ṣaff*, *O you who have faith! Why do you that which you do not do? Most loathsome is it in the sight of God that you say that which you do not do* (Q. 61:2–3). Similarly, the noble Messenger ﷺ said,

> A man will be brought on the Day of Resurrection and will be cast into Hell, and his intestines will pour forth and he will go round them as a donkey goes round a millstone. The inmates of Hell will gather round him and say: "What has happened to you, O so-and-so? Were you not enjoining us to do good and forbidding us to do evil?" He will reply: "I was enjoining you to do good, but was not doing it myself; and I was forbidding you to do evil, but was doing it myself."[1]

One of the great preachers of the past, Yaḥyā b. Muʿādh al-Rāzī (d. 258/872), once said in poetic verse,

> The exhortation of the preacher will never be accepted
> until he himself takes it to heart.
> O people! Who is more evil than a preacher
> who violates his own public exhortations?
> In public he makes a display of his good deeds,
> but in private he does battle against the Merciful One.[2]

Given these heavy reminders, it is essential that an Islamic preacher be rooted in spiritual truth and ethical behavior that stems from God-consciousness for the goodness of themselves and for the goodness of the community. As Christian scholar Arthur Hoyt observes in his book *The Preacher*, "A man can never be separated from his speech."[3]

Furthermore, the stature of the *khaṭīb*—that of standing on the pulpit before a congregation—is a position of great influence and authority within the community. Inevitably, the congregation comes to view, at the very least, their regular *khaṭīb* as a minimalist religious scholar, meaning one who is able to answer Islamic legal questions (*fiqh*) and offer wise counsel (*naṣīḥa*) and is expected to model good behavior (*adab wa-akhlāq*). Ibn al-Jawzī reflects on this reality of a preacher's life:

> Only the learned man (*'ālim*) who is firmly rooted in all the branches of knowledge should narrate stories (*yaquṣṣu*) [or preach], for he will be asked to discourse in each of these fields. The jurisconsult (*faqīh*) is scarcely even questioned about matters relating to the science of tradition when he conducts a course in law, nor is the expert in tradition (*muḥaddith*) very often asked about matters relating to law. The preacher (*wā'iẓ*), on the other hand, is questioned concerning every field of knowledge. For this reason it is necessary to be a perfectly learned man. . . . All of the preceding qualifications, however, hinge upon fear (*taqwā*) of God, for the impact of [the preacher's] words will be in direct relation to his fear of God. One of the pious men of old once said: "Whenever exhortation issues from the heart of an upright man it makes an impression on the hearts of those who hear it. This proves that his intention is pure, for when his intention is pure God causes the people to respond to him and eradicates from his heart any desire for their wealth."[4]

All of this is to say that it is important for us, in this guide and beyond, to reflect on the life and character of an Islamic preacher.

This chapter is devoted to four essential aspects of a preacher's life, aspects that greatly influence the reach and effectiveness of a preacher. Namely, we will focus on the spiritual, intellectual, social, and physical aspects of a preacher's life and development. The explanations of these aspects are meant to be aspirational, not descriptive. In other words, a preacher hopes and struggles for these lofty characteristics over the course of their lifetime, and they are not to be expected in their fullness from the outset.

Spiritual Life and Character

The two most important spiritual states that a preacher must constantly struggle to attain are God-consciousness (*taqwā*) and sincerity (*ikhlāṣ*). *Taqwā* means awareness of God's complete knowledge of your inward state and outward behavior and of God's omnipresence in your life. God-consciousness is what prevents abuse of stature and motivates you to be diligent in performing your preaching duties responsibly. Allah the Honorable says in *surāt āl 'Imrān, O you who have faith! Be conscious of God with all the consciousness that is His due and die not unless you have surrendered [to Him]* (Q. 3:102). It is said that Ali, may God ennoble his face, once came across a preacher in the marketplace and warned him against preaching out of ignorance. Then Ali said to the preacher,

> "I am going to ask you a question! If you answer what I ask, well and good! Otherwise I will chastise you!" The preacher replied: "Ask whatever you like, O Commander of the Faithful!" So 'Alī asked: "What upholds faith (*īmān*), and what destroys it?" The preacher replied: "That which upholds faith is conscientiousness (*wara'*), and that which destroys it is greediness (*ṭama'*)." 'Alī answered: "People like you ought to preach!"[5]

The place of *taqwā* is in the heart, and its manifestation is in the limbs—particularly the tongue, which is known in Islamic spirituality as the mirror of the heart. Thus, the attainment of *taqwā* is in constantly nourishing and safeguarding the heart with the remembrance of God. Furthermore, the vessels to the heart are seven: the ears, eyes, tongue, stomach, private parts, hands, and feet. These vessels give spiritual life to the heart through prayer (*ṣalāt*), night vigil (*qiyyām*), recollection (*dhikr*), fasting (*siyyām*), and preoccupation with good works such as charity (*ṣadaqa*). These vessels are constricted and deprive the heart of spiritual life through heedlessness (*ghafla*) and disobedience (*'iṣyān*).

Gaining true sincerity is probably one of the major obstacles in the spiritual life of a preacher with praise and position directed toward the pulpit. *Ikhlāṣ* is developed with the theological understanding of God's Reality and our reality in relation to the Real (*al-haqq*). Once our hearts and minds comprehend the awe that is due to God, then all other motivations—wealth, status, praise, and the like—disappear. It should suffice for the preacher to know that as the Beloved of God ﷺ said, "Allah looks not at your figures, nor at your outward appearance but He looks at your hearts and deeds."[6] Imam al-Ghazālī offers a definition of sincerity and a cure for insincerity in *Letter to a Disciple*:

> You questioned me about sincerity. It is that all your deeds be for God the Exalted, and that your heart be not gladdened by men's praises nor that you care about their censure. Know that insincerity is produced by overestimating mankind. The cure for it is for you to see them as subject to omnipotence, and for you to reckon them as though inanimate objects, powerless to bestow ease or hardship, so you become free of insincerity towards them. As long as you reckon them as having control and free-will, insincerity will not keep away from you.[7]

Thank God, then, for all the hardships associated with a preacher's life—these difficulties, which make a preacher's life less attractive and glamorous, are a gift from Allah the Compassionate to keep us sincere!

What has been said here regarding the attainment of *taqwā* and *ikhlāṣ* is sufficient, and to say more would be to digress from our main topic. I would recommend following up with the guidance provided by the sages of our religion, such as al-Ghazālī and *The Beginning of Guidance* (*Bidāyat al-hidāya*), and by the faith-oriented perspectives raised by more contemporaneous works such as *The Agenda to Change Our Condition* by Shaykh Hamza Yusuf and Imam Zaid Shakir; *Science of the Cosmos, Science of the Soul: The Pertinence of Islamic Cosmology in the Modern World* by William C. Chittick; and *Rethinking Islam and the West* by Ahmed Paul Keeler.[8]

Our spiritual states are directly related to our outward behavior and character so that the two must go arm in arm. Whether we like it or not, accept it or not, preachers are often seen as the model for proper behavior and character in a community. Thus, our outward behavior not only affects who we are with Allah the All-Knowing but also affects the effectiveness of our preaching and leading. This is not to say that only the saintly should preach, but it must be the arduous desire and objective of every preacher to reach a state of inward and outward character that is worthy of the Prophet's pulpit. And for every beautiful quality desired in a preacher we have a beautiful model in the Messenger of Allah ﷺ,

who was "sent only to perfect noble character," according to a well-known hadith.[9] The following seven virtues are essential characteristics of a good preacher.

1. Truthfulness (*ṣidq*)

A preacher's words are only powerful and moving if his speech is known to be truthful and honorable. It is no coincidence that the Prophet ﷺ first became known to his people as *al-Amīn*, or "the trustworthy one," before he was known as a prophet and preacher. Allah the Real says in *sūrat al-tawba, O you who have faith! Be conscious of God and be among the truthful* (Q. 9:119). Similarly, in *sūrat al-aḥzāb, O you who have faith! Be conscious of God and speak rightly* (Q. 33:70). The Prophet ﷺ also encouraged the virtue of truthfulness by saying, "Truth leads to piety and piety leads to paradise. A man persists in speaking the truth till he is enrolled with Allah as a truthful one (*ṣiddīq*)."[10] At the very least, being truthful in the context of preaching means never speaking a lie from the pulpit and being diligent in ascertaining the truth of stories, especially hadiths, before relaying them to the congregation. It should cause enough fear in the heart of a preacher to know that the Prophet ﷺ said, "Whoever tells a lie against me, then let him prepare for his seat in Hell."[11] If one is unsure of the authenticity of any hadith or story but nonetheless seeks to draw wisdom from it, then it is best to convey that doubt of authenticity to the community of listeners. The congregation places enormous trust in the preacher and the stories or prophetic narrations that he cites, so be careful in this matter. To be truthful, one should also avoid pretentiousness in all its forms, such as fake weeping or the like. Speaking truth, in its highest form, means speaking truth to power. In a democracy, power—at least to some extent—lies with the people. As such, preachers need to articulate hard and uncomfortable truths to the people of their congregations with courage and wisdom.

2. Courage (*shajāʿa*)

Speaking the truth may not always be as easy as it seems. At times, speaking the truth requires courage and certitude about what is right, good, and just even if it leads to criticism from others or institutional censure. Prolonged silence may lead to complicity in wrong and giving aid to falsehood. In the words of Dr. Martin Luther King Jr., "There comes a time when silence is betrayal"[12] and "we will have to repent . . . not merely from the loud and bitter words of the bad people but for the appalling silence of the good people."[13] These are deep words for a preacher to reflect on. And as we prepare our sermons, we have to ask ourselves if we are speaking the truths that need to be spoken and if we are—with our words—inspiring people to witness to the truth. Hoyt writes beautifully about this virtue of courage: "The preacher needs to be a *brave man* who can face men and danger unflinchingly. . . . He speaks the truth in love, but he speaks the truth at any cost. He is able to espouse an unpopular but righteous cause. Courage is the superb asset of the preacher. Without it men will not long respect his word."[14]

3. Wisdom (*ḥikma*)

Of course, not every truth is to be spoken at every moment, and knowing when to speak only comes from wisdom. For the preacher, knowing when to speak, what to speak, and how to speak constitutes real wisdom. Therefore, preachers must never speak from their passions, even when conveying a truth, without carefully considering the objective and how best to achieve that objective. Wisdom also requires that a preacher learn how to speak of the universal essence of matters rather than getting caught up in the details. Imam al-Ghazālī writes about the one blessed with wisdom, "Indeed the discourse of one who knows God is different from that of others. Rarely does he concern himself with particulars; he rather speaks of matters universal in scope."[15] As such, the wisest words uttered by the wisest people are ones that have a universal appeal and ones that inspire people long after the wise have spoken them. Consider, for example, the words of someone like Malcolm X, may God rest his soul, which continue to inspire people to the light of Islam.

4. Compassion and Love (*raḥma wa-mawadda*)

Every prophet that was sent by God was sent with a compassionate and loving heart and preached to his people with utmost goodwill, desiring only that they find everlasting happiness and success in turning to God. Thus the Prophet ﷺ said, in what is considered by scholars to be the foundational hadith on which our very Islamic tradition is based, that "people who show mercy to others will be shown mercy by the All-Merciful. Be merciful to those on earth, and He who is in heaven will be merciful to you."[16] If we want our preaching to be a blessing for ourselves and for our community, then possessing this quality of compassionate love is essential. Again, in the words of Hoyt, "A *sympathetic nature* should be the gift of the preacher; a power to feel with men and touch the cords of the human heart. . . . To enter into the experiences of another life, to read noble possibilities behind rough faces and hard conditions, gives to preaching that humanity which is its most attractive and persuasive quality."[17] Even when a sermon is delivered with fierce urgency, it must stem from a compassionate-loving disposition, as one would urge people to flee a burning house out of genuine care and concern. Imam al-Ghazālī, quite remarkably, reflects on this characteristic of a compassionate and loving person who is awestruck by Allah the Compassionate-Loving in his book *The Ninety-Nine Beautiful Names of God*:

> Man's share in the name *al-Raḥmān* lies in his showing mercy to the negligent, dissuading them from the path of negligence towards God—great and glorious—by exhortation and counseling, by way of gentleness not violence, regarding the disobedient with eyes of mercy and not contempt; letting every insubordination perpetrated in the world be as his own misfortune, so sparing no effort to eliminate it to the extent that he can—all out of mercy to the disobedient lest they be exposed to God's wrath and so deserve to be removed from proximity to Him.[18]

5. Patience (*ṣabr*)

The fruits of preaching take time—sometimes years, decades, and even centuries—to manifest themselves in the hearts, actions, and social realities of a people. Many of the greatest preachers in the world, Muslim and non-Muslim, did not even see the full impact of their preaching during their lifetime. The Messenger ﷺ himself endured much hardship during his life as a prophet and preacher and was only able to endure with the might of patient perseverance. *Truly God is with those who patiently persevere* (Q. 2:153), says Allah the Patient in *sūrat al-baqara*. A preacher can easily become frustrated when they do not see change immediately. Patience, therefore, is an invaluable companion in the life journey of a preacher.

6. Humility (*tawāḍu'*)

A preacher must never preach or act with even the slightest hint of arrogance. Such a preacher is not only in an awful state with God but also an ineffective preacher in the long run. It should suffice the preacher to know, as the Beloved of Allah ﷺ said, that "the one who possesses even an atom's weight of arrogance shall not enter paradise."[19] Arrogance is one of the most dangerous obstacles that a preacher faces with praise and respect directed toward the one who stands on the pulpit. And humility can be a difficult trait to attain when week after week the preacher is preaching to people. The preacher can easily become deluded into thinking that their words on the pulpit are sufficient for their own deeds. Caliph Umar, may God be pleased with him, once advised a man who was considering preaching, "I fear for you if you [preach]. You will first come to consider yourself above the people. . . . Moreover, your self-esteem will rise to the point where you will imagine that you are as high above them in rank as the Pleiades. However, God will put you under their feet on the Day of Resurrection in the measure in which you esteem yourself above them."[20]

The hearts of people are opened to divine light through humility and softness and are deterred by arrogance and harshness. In *sūrat al-shuʿarāʾ*, Allah the Sublime advises his own Beloved ﷺ, *And lower your wings of kindness over all the believers who may follow you* (Q. 26:215). This kindness comes only out of a spirit of humbleness—the lowering of one's wings—a spirit that the greatest preachers have always possessed. A good piece of advice that a teacher once gave me many years ago was to always preach knowing that the one most in need of a reminder is oneself and to know that any shortcomings that I possess are inexcusable, while those to whom I preach have the excuse of unawareness for any of their shortcomings. In this way, humility is acquired and made manifest in our preaching.

7. Modesty (*ḥayāʾ*)

A quality of humility is modesty—a shyness and simplicity that appear in our speech, appearance, and mannerisms. The Messenger ﷺ, who was himself described as being the most modest of men, said, "Modesty only brings good."[21] Ibn al-Jawzī reflects extensively on the importance of modesty and simplicity:

> It is important for the preacher (*wāʿiẓ*) that he give up the luxuries of life and garb himself in modest clothes in order that he might become an example for others to follow. ʿUmar b. al-Khaṭṭāb's *izār* (outer garment) had numerous patches on it. ʿAlī b. Abī Ṭālib used to clothe himself in garments of an inferior quality. Someone once asked him about that and he replied: "[I do this] so that Muslims may emulate me." Now [the validity of] this is illustrated by the fact that when the physician himself abstains from things which are injurious to the health his prescriptions to others to do

> so are effective, but when he takes such things his commands to others to abstain do no good. Abū'l-Wafā' b. 'Aqīl said: "For every kind of utterance there is an appropriate exterior aspect . . . preaching (*wa'ẓ*) is to be carried out in accordance with the principles of asceticism by means of a woolen garment (meaning a simple garment), an emaciated body, the consuming of small quantities of food, thus distracting the mind away from the body and preoccupying it with the excellences of the spirit."[22]

Ibn al-Jawzī is pointing to another very important quality of the preacher, which is tied to the quality of modesty: that of *moderation* (*ṣadad*) in every aspect of behavior. We know that the Prophet ﷺ was a perfectly balanced human being, from the way he laughed to the way he ate and even in his religious devotions. In an age of extremes, moderation is a quality that preachers must embody as an antithesis to one of the greatest challenges of our time. Another important aspect of modesty is found in respectful gender interactions. The preacher must be careful to interact with the opposite gender in a dignified manner that is devoid of any hints of flirtation or the like. The young preacher must be particularly careful to restrain the charisma and charm that often naturally come with their position.[23]

Interestingly, the word *ḥayā'* is also tied to the word *ḥayāh*, which means "life." Both are derived from the same root in Arabic. We can discern an intimate connection between these two concepts. It can be said, then, that humbleness and modesty give life to the words that we speak from the pulpit—life that awakens the hearts of believers to the true purpose of life and to God the Living. As God says in *sūrat al-furqān*, *And trust in the Living, Who never dies and glorify His praise* (Q. 25:58).

Intellectual Life

A preacher can only serve as a vessel of knowledge for their community if they are in constant pursuit of learning. One of the hallmarks of a great preacher is their love of knowledge. It is no coincidence that the very first verse revealed to God's Messenger ﷺ was *Read! In the name of your Lord, who created* (Q. 96:1). And in a well-known hadith, the Prophet ﷺ commanded the believers, "Seeking knowledge is obligatory upon every Muslim."[24] In the introduction to this chapter, we cited Ibn al-Jawzī's high expectation of the knowledge base of a preacher.

Hashem reasserts this idea in his research by stating that "the Muslim tradition contains an expectation of a little *'alim* [religious scholar] in every *khatib*."[25]

A person who is asked to preach consistently will find that it is only their knowledge bank that can keep their sermons lively and refreshing as opposed to dull and routine. Furthermore, a *khaṭīb* should be prepared to address people's questions outside of a *khuṭba*. I personally have encountered numerous occasions when someone from the congregation wanted to ask me a religious question after the *khuṭba*, usually on a topic completely different from the *khuṭba* itself. Now, this does not mean that a *khaṭīb* must answer every question he receives if he is not confident about the answer. As the example of Imam Mālik b. Anas (d. 179/795) attests, despite his learning, he would not shy away from responding to questions with the humble reply, "I do not know."[26] According to Abū Bakr al-Bayhaqī (d. 458/1066), Ibn 'Abbās would say that "'I do not know' is half of knowledge."[27] Indeed, the sounder and more honorable thing to do is to direct people's questions to those who do know.

Nevertheless, a preacher should strive to gain knowledge for themselves. The pursuit of knowledge is a most blessed pursuit and surely, God willing, an immense benefit for the community. It is important for the *khaṭīb* to strive for expertise in the following essential branches of knowledge.

1. The Qur'an

Our scripture contains knowledge and wisdom as vast as all of the oceans of the world. Every science in Islam springs forth from the Qur'an. Each field of knowledge is nourished by it. As such, a daily disciplined study of the Qur'an, outside of preparing for a *khuṭba*, is vital for every good Islamic preacher. Studying the Qur'an means acquiring its proper recitation (*tajwīd*), memorization (*ḥifẓ*), explanation (*tafsīr*), and application (*ḥikma*). For a sermon to be pleasing to the hearts of a congregation and for the preacher to have any legitimacy in the eyes of the community, a correct and beautiful reading of the Qur'an is needed. There is nothing that takes the air out of a sermon more than a preacher stumbling over a Qur'anic citation. The best way to learn *tajwīd* is by sitting with an expert teacher who corrects and enhances the recitation. Listening frequently to master Qur'an reciters can improve one's own recitation. Memorization allows a preacher to draw appropriately from the ocean of the Qur'an for every topic and occasion. The art of memorization requires strict discipline and clear goals that are to be achieved in a specific period of time. Begin by memorizing those passages that you find yourself drawing on frequently in your sermons.

Understanding and contemplating the Qur'an requires serious commitment. This *umma* has been blessed with men and women who have dedicated their entire lives to Qur'anic commentary and interpretation. Drink, then, from these wells of knowledge that have been left behind and are continuing to be built as we speak! Reading and reflecting on these commentaries deepens our own understanding of scripture, and the mark of this is seen immediately and directly in the content of our preaching. Perhaps the most important task for the preacher is to learn how to read the Qur'an—with the aid of a study group and one's own reflecting—in a way that brings to life the passages of the Qur'an and gives relevance to the here and now. As preachers, we have the responsibility to show people how the Qur'anic message is still as meaningful to our lives as it was for the original community more than fourteen hundred years ago. To achieve this purpose, I recommend keeping a Qur'an journal in which you write down your daily thoughts and that which you learn from others about the meanings contained in the scripture. You will find that many of these journal reflection entries will form the backbone of your most successful sermons.

Recommended Readings

- Sohaib Sultan, *The Qur'an and Sayings of the Prophet Muhammad: Selections Annotated and Explained* (Woodstock, VT: SkyLight Illuminations, 2007).
- Ingrid Mattson, *The Story of the Qur'an: Its History and Place in Muslim Life* (Malden, MA: Blackwell, 2008).
- Celene Ibrahim, *Women and Gender in the Qur'an* (New York: Oxford University Press, 2020).

2. The Sayings, Character, and Life of the Prophet ﷺ

It is essential for preachers to be intimately familiar and in love with the prophetic way culminating in the *Sunna* of the Messenger of Allah ﷺ. This means being well acquainted with the Prophet's traditions (*ḥadīth*), his general life (*sīra*), and the portrait of his character (*shamā'il*). If our purpose is to guide people to a God-conscious life and good deeds, then what better model to draw on than the Beloved of Allah ﷺ? But we are only in a position to draw on the model of the Best of Creation ﷺ if we are dedicated students of his noble path. Like the Qur'an, it is our responsibility as preachers to bring to life the prophetic path and make it as relevant as it has always been for the *umma*. There are several books to draw on to study the life and character of the Prophet ﷺ, and different preachers will find appeal in different versions. One of the greatest books in our possession is the collection by Imam al-Nawawī (d. 676/1277) entitled *Riyāḍ al-Ṣāliḥīn* ("The Gardens of the Righteous"), which is a beautiful compilation of the Prophet's teachings and details about his character. A preacher would do well to become intimately familiar with *The Garden of the Righteous* and internalize many of the traditions found therein through memorization and actualization.

Recommended Readings

- Martin Lings, *Muhammad: His Life Based on the Earliest Sources* (Rochester, VT: Inner Traditions International, 1983).
- Shaykh Yusuf Nabahani, *Muhammad: His Character and Beauty—Wasa'il al-Wusul ila Shama'il al-Rasul*, trans. Abdul Aziz Suraqah (Al-Madina Institute, 2015).
- Meraj Mohiuddin, *Revelation: The Story of Muhammad, Peace and Blessings Be upon Him* (Scottsdale, AZ: Whiteboard, 2016).

3. Theology

Beyond the need for an Islamic preacher to know and understand the Islamic creed (*arkān al-īmān*), there are times when a preacher is faced with situations or questions that raise trying theological questions, such as widespread suffering in the midst of a natural disaster. Today, there is even skepticism over the existence of God and thus about the validity of religion altogether. Atheism has succeeded in leading many people away from God often through appeals to science. None of these challenges is insurmountable by any means, but addressing them does require serious study and thought. In my experience, the few times that theology has ever been addressed in a sermon, it is often focused on theological minutiae for which there are wide differences of opinion and that are typically irrelevant to the lives of listeners. Nevertheless, the theology that is relevant to people's lives and concerns is too often overlooked in our sermons. Books such as *Islam and the Problem of Black Suffering* by Sherman Jackson must become mandatory reading for Islamic preachers today.[28]

Recommended Readings

- Sachiko Murata and William C. Chittick, *The Vision of Islam* (St. Paul, MN: Paragon House, 1994).
- Martin Nguyen, *Modern Muslim Theology: Engaging God and the World with Faith and Imagination* (Lanham, MD: Rowman & Littlefield, 2019).

4. Law and Ethics

The vast science of *sharīʿa*, which forms the code of life for a believer, is one of the most beautiful hallmarks of this religion. Its study elucidates for us religious practice as well as ethical and moral life. It is not necessary for every preacher to be a *faqīh*, or a specialist in Islamic law, but it is necessary for every preacher to know and understand the general principles by which the *sharīʿa* shapes human life. The deeper our understanding of the *sharīʿa*, the deeper our sermon's content and effectiveness. As we noted earlier, in the life of a preacher it is very beneficial to master at least core aspects of Islamic law. At the very least, though, the *khaṭīb* should be in touch and have established contacts with one or more Islamic legal scholars so that they might be able to help answer some of the questions that will come their way.

Recommended Readings

- Ahmad ibn Naqib al-Misri, *Reliance of the Traveller: A Classical Manual of Islamic Sacred Law*, rev. ed., trans. Nuh Ha Mim Keller (Beltsville, MD: Amana, 1994).
- Mohammed Hashim Kamali, *Shari'ah Law: An Introduction* (Oxford: Oneworld, 2008).

5. The Spiritual Sciences

A wise preacher not only identifies problems in the human condition but also offers medicine for these ailments. A good preacher understands the root of spiritual diseases that manifest themselves in all sorts of evils from excessive corporate greed to inhumane bloodshed. Our spiritual sciences were developed to offer the cure for exactly those root spiritual problems. These guides, which are found in hundreds of books, should be part of the daily reading that we engage with for our own benefit, since the preacher is often most in need of these remedies. Moreover, because the spiritual sciences help us develop our own souls, they will necessarily become a part of what we preach and how we preach. While there are many texts to consult, the magisterial work by Imam al-Ghazālī known as *Iḥyā ʿulūm al-dīn*, or "The Revival of the Religious Sciences," is especially insightful, and many of its books have been translated into English by Fons Vitae and the Islamic Texts Society.

Recommended Readings

- Muhammad Emin Er, *Laws of the Heart: An Introduction to the Spiritual Path in Islam*, trans. Joseph Walsh (Atlanta: Shifa, 2008).
- Yasmin Mogahed, *Reclaim Your Heart: Personal Insights on Breaking Free from Life's Shackles* (San Clemente, CA: FB Publishing, 2012).
- A. Helwa, *Secrets of Divine Love: A Spiritual Journey into the Heart of Islam* (Capistrano Beach, CA: Naulit, 2020).

6. History

People learn best through stories. Some of the best stories are of past peoples—their successes, challenges, and failures. Study in depth the early Muslim community, the scholars and thinkers who shaped the Islamic tradition, and the makers of history who spread Islam to the farthest corners of the world. There is much wisdom to gain from these people and their times. One caution, however, is to avoid romanticizing Islamic history, which all too often occurs in preaching. There is undoubtedly greatness and glory in our history, but when we forget that our history was also marred with human discord and corruption, we present an unachievable and unrealistic expectation of what can be. When young people are introduced to a more critical study of Islamic history, as opposed to the overembellished versions often found in our uncritical preaching and weekend schools, they are often crushed to discover that Islamic history offers no escape from the reality of human vices. Again, when young people are presented with this unreal, idealized version of history, it is easy for them to become depressed by and frustrated with the current state of affairs and to become disillusioned with the world. Islamic history, even its troubling parts, has much to teach us if we would only appreciate the fullness of the human experience, both its good and bad.

Recommended Readings

- Jonathan P. Berkey, *The Formation of Islam: Religion and Society in the Near East, 600–1800* (Cambridge: Cambridge University Press, 2003).

- Michael Hamilton Morgan, *Lost History: The Enduring Legacy of Muslim Scientists, Thinkers, and Artists* (Washington, DC: National Geographic, 2007).
- Edward E. Curtis IV, *Muslims in America: A Short History* (Oxford: Oxford University Press, 2009).
- Sylvia Chan-Malik, *Being Muslim: A Cultural History of Women of Color in American Islam* (New York: New York University Press, 2018).

7. Language

It is necessary for the Islamic preacher to have at least a decent command of Arabic. Knowledge of Arabic gives the preacher direct access to the primary sources of Islam and to a vast collection of resources from the Islamic tradition. Knowing the deeper root meanings of Arabic words—especially key concepts—can further illuminate a sermon. English is also a necessary language for the American *khaṭīb* to master. In the most beautiful and wise of ways, preaching requires that the preacher has full command of the language in which they are to preach. It is no coincidence that Malcolm X methodically studied the entire English dictionary before becoming the great preacher that he was.[29]

Recommended Reading

- Malcolm X, *Malcolm X Speaks: Selected Speeches and Statements*, ed. George Breitman (New York: Grove, 1965).

Apart from these essential branches of knowledge, there are other beneficial fields of learning that can potentially aid the preacher in preparing and delivering good sermons.

8. Psychology and Counseling

Much of the task of the preacher is to motivate members of a congregation toward goodness and away from vice. Knowing how the human mind processes information, how feelings are evoked from the spoken word, and what motivates people toward a particular objective is all studied in the field of psychology. Understanding psychology can help a preacher communicate their message more effectively. Gaining competency in the field of counseling is beneficial for the preacher, and it helps with preaching that is counseling based (see chapter 1). It is also the case that a preacher will inevitably be asked to serve as a counselor on certain occasions. Learning how to listen with compassion and how to be a caring presence in people's lives is a valuable trait that the field of counseling can develop in a preacher.

Recommended Readings

- Sameera Ahmed and Mona M. Amer, eds., *Counseling Muslims: Handbook of Mental Health Issues and Interventions* (New York: Routledge, 2012).
- Mikaeel Ahmed Smith, *With the Heart in Mind: The Moral and Emotional Intelligence of the Prophet (S)* (Qasim, 2019).
- Salma Abugideiri and Mohamed Hag Magid, *Before You Tie the Knot: A Guide for Couples* (Self-published, CreateSpace: 2014).

9. Sociology

This field focuses on the forces that shape societies, how societies function, and how identity is formed within certain groups in a society. This knowledge can be beneficial for the social-preacher who seeks to cultivate certain qualities in a community and seeks to shape communal identity. It is also important for a preacher to be aware of the various social forces that have shaped and are shaping the larger society of which Muslims are a part. Identifying these social forces and understanding how they affect people's lives can help a preacher communicate to the masses more effectively. The Islamic preacher can also play a role in helping newly arrived Muslim communities make sense of American society. Sociology can aid the preacher in fulfilling this role.

Recommended Readings

- Atul Gawande, *Being Mortal: Medicine and What Matters in the End* (New York: Metropolitan, 2014).
- John Palfrey and Urs Gasser, *Born Digital: How Children Grow Up in a Digital Age*, rev. and expanded ed. (New York: Basic Books, 2016).
- Beverly Daniel Tatum, *Why Are All the Black Kids Sitting Together in the Cafeteria? and Other Conversations about Race*, 20th anniversary ed. (New York: Basic Books, 2017).

10. World Religions

Living in the pluralistic society that we do, it is important for an Islamic preacher to have some basic understanding of other religions. Such knowledge is beneficial in two ways. First, if people from another faith tradition come to visit the site of a sermon, the preacher may be able to shape the content of his sermon in a way that is relatable and embracing of the guests. Second, a preacher is often called upon to answer questions from non-Muslims or give lectures at interfaith gatherings. Knowing what others believe and practice may aid the Islamic preacher in this task.

Recommended Readings

- John Renard, *Islam and Christianity: Theological Themes in Comparative Perspective* (Berkeley: University of California Press, 2011).
- Reza Shah-Kazemi, *The Spirit of Tolerance in Islam* (London: I. B. Tauris, 2012).

11. Current Affairs and Contemporary Challenges

One of the chief characteristics of good preachers is that they remain relevant. In other words, a preacher should be in tune with the concerns of the congregation and not cut off from them. Only when the preacher knows what is on the minds of people will they able to preach to their concerns. Nonetheless, the preacher needs to be cognizant of the fact that what social media and the twenty-four-hour news cycle put out as "current affairs" may not really be the "current affairs" on people's minds. A relevant preacher should have access to a wide range of sources to broaden their scope and perspective concerning what is happening in the world. Moreover, the preacher must be in touch with the average person in order to know what truly concerns and worries them. In seeking such knowledge, the preacher must be clear that the objective is not to gain information but rather to grow in openmindedness and openheartedness in order to nurture faith. In the words of Hoyt, "Knowledge must be transformed by experience into *spiritual wisdom*. It must help the preacher to live and so help others to live."[30]

Recommended Readings

- Ibrahim Abdul-Matin, *Green Deen: What Islam Teaches about Protecting the Planet* (San Francisco: Berrett-Koehler, 2010).
- Jonathan A. C. Brown, *Misquoting Muhammad: The Challenge and Choices of Interpreting the Prophet's Legacy* (London: Oneworld, 2014).
- Juliane Hammer, *Peaceful Families: American Muslim Efforts against Domestic Violence* (Princeton, NJ: Princeton University Press, 2019).

Social Life

A preacher faces a delicate balance of being *with* the people without becoming *of* the people. In other words, the preacher that is completely removed from their community is considered aloof and rendered ineffective. Yet a preacher who is overly immersed in the life of a community risks losing that aura of dignity and respect that is naturally attached to a preacher and that is helpful in preaching. Hoyt writes about the importance of a preacher being with the people: "We are to be men in spiritual life, not angels; in touch with men, not above them. Not preaching an isolated and repellent piety, but bringing the world of heavenly ideals and inspirations into the life of the common day."[31] Ibn al-Jawzī, on the other hand, offers a counter-perspective, effectively warning the preacher from spending too much time with the people. He writes, "It is of particular importance that [the preacher] refrain from mixing with the people and that he appear as a pious and sober person when he conducts his public exhortation; when he mixes with the people and jokes with them they will lose their respect for him."[32]

The proper course, I believe, lies in between or in moderation. If we look to the Prophetic model, we see someone who enjoyed the company of his companions, who laughed at their jokes and also joked with them. At the same time, the manner of the Prophet ﷺ was always dignified and balanced. Even when he laughed, it would only be so much as a wide smile. That was the nature of the blessed Prophet ﷺ. His model is here for us to emulate. Nevertheless, this is a legitimate point of consideration: how much time should the preacher spend with his community if they do not yet possess such prophetic qualities? A preacher must consider that in the eyes of many, they are a role model. Therefore, a preacher's interaction and discourse with the people are not the same as those of others. If the preacher models less-than-appropriate behavior in social interactions, then it is likely that the people will follow suit, even if the preacher amends his behavior in the future. All of this is not to dissuade the preacher from associating with people entirely but rather to burden the preacher with the responsibility of modeling goodness in social life.

Imam al-Ghazālī sets a high bar for the proper interaction of preachers in society. He writes, "Whenever you interact with people, deal with them as you would wish yourself to be dealt with by them, for a worshipper's faith is incomplete until he wants for other people what he wants for himself."[33] This advice, of course, is based on the prophetic counsel, "No one is a true believer until he desires for his brother what he desires for himself."[34] Imam al-Nawawī and others have commented that the "brother" mentioned in the hadith means brother in humanity, not only in faith. Realistically, of course, most American Muslim preachers are lay preachers. As lay preachers, there is no alternative but to be with the people either as coworkers, classmates, or the like. Such interactions, then, are opportunities to bring, in the words of Hoyt, "heavenly ideals" to the fabric of society. For our social interactions to be good and wholesome, preachers—no matter how busy—must first make the time to take care of our spiritual, intellectual, and physical selves.

Physical Life

It is no secret that the life of an Islamic preacher is full of pressures and demands, some of which are related to the preaching vocation and others that are associated with the challenging life of a preacher. Some of these pressures and demands are natural, while others are born out of a savior complex. Regardless, the preacher needs to take control of their physical life in order to be effective, especially in the long term. Health and time management, then, must be made priorities in the life of a preacher.

Health

In an oft-quoted hadith, the Prophet ﷺ said that "your body has a right over you."[35] This means that taking care of one's physical health is just as important as taking care of other people. If we only use reason, the one who does not take care of themselves will not be able to take care of the needs of others for long. A preacher who is not physically well will find it difficult to preach with the enthusiasm, passion, and voice that is needed to awaken people's hearts. As Hoyt writes, "However lofty the purpose and pure the love, a weak and sickly body will make the work drag heavily."[36] Taking care of one's health requires proper diet, exercise, and rest.

The best advice on proper diet comes from the Messenger ﷺ, who said that "no man fills a vessel worse than his stomach. A few morsels that keep his back straight are sufficient for the children of Adam. If [more than this] is necessary, then he should fill one-third with food, one-third with drink, and leave one-third for easy breathing."[37] This hadith reflects the Qur'anic counsel: *O children of Adam . . . eat and drink, but not excessively, for [God] loves not the excessive* (Q. 7:31).

If one eats the right amount without indulging beyond what is needed, they will find an abundance of energy to fulfill life's various tasks. Exercise also maintains one's health and energizes the body for a long day's work. The Prophet ﷺ encouraged engaging in sports, and there are reports that he would run with his wife. Hoyt writes that "play is no less divine than work"[38] and advises that a preacher reserve at least half an hour every day for exercise that rejuvenates the body. It is an excellent way to begin one's day after morning worship.

Finally, the right amount of rest keeps the mind alert and the body ready for the hard work of preaching. The Prophet ﷺ would arrange his typical day in such a manner as to reserve eight hours for rest and relaxation. Resting for the sake of the lower appetites is a fault, but resting so that one may have the energy to serve Allah is in itself an act of worship. Many a preacher deludes themselves into thinking that the longer they stay up at night, the more they will get done. However, studies and experience have shown that the most efficient hours for work are usually the early morning hours after a good night's rest.

Time Management

The most important word in the English language that a preacher must learn to use is the word *no*. Undoubtedly, there is an incredible amount of demand from the community on a preacher's time. But this is partly because many preachers have not learned how to choose engagements carefully and wisely. Not every invitation or opportunity that comes a preacher's way should be accepted. Be humble and trusting enough to pass on engagements or opportunities to others.

What is also needed is maintaining a strict daily schedule that balances life and work. Imam al-Ghazālī offers wise advice on this matter:

> Your time should not be without any structure, such that you occupy yourself arbitrarily with whatever comes along. Rather, you must take account of yourself and order your worship during the day and the night, assigning to each period of time an activity that must not be neglected nor replaced by another activity. By this ordering of time, the blessing in time will show itself. A person who leaves himself without a plan as animals do, not knowing what he is to do at any given moment, will spend most of his time fruitlessly. Your time is your life, and your life is your capital: by it you make your trade, and by it you will reach the eternal bounties in

> the proximity of Allāh. Every single breath of yours is a priceless jewel because it is irreplaceable; once it is gone, there is no return for it. So do not be like fools who rejoice each day as their wealth increases while their lives decrease. What good is there in wealth that increases while one's lifespan decreases? Do not rejoice except in an increase of knowledge or an increase of good works. Truly they are your two friends who will accompany you in your grave, when your spouse, your wealth, your children, and your friends will remain behind.[39]

It is reported that the Prophet ﷺ would divide his time into three eight-hour portions: one-third for worship; one-third for work; and one-third for family, friends, and relaxation. What is needed in the schedule of a preacher is balance. There must be time for work, but there must also be time for worship, self-care, and family duties. A preacher's family has as much claim on them as the community. Beware of what Christian ministers refer to as the problem of "righteous adultery," meaning that one completely neglects their spouse for the sake of work. Time management, thus, is the key to a successful preaching life.

• • •

In this chapter, we have paused to reflect on a preacher's life, which inevitably affects their preaching. What we have described here might sound daunting, but that is not the intention. This religion is a religion of high aspiration (*himma ʿāliyya*). As such, we should aspire for our preaching to be the best of preaching and our preachers to be the best of preachers. This requires setting the bar high and then struggling hard to meet those expectations. The key is to see the ideal qualities of a preacher—mentioned in this chapter and beyond—as something to aspire to over a lifetime, not as a description of what a preacher is expected to be like from the beginning. There are times when the preacher, in their self-development, will falter or fall short. Nonetheless, know that imperfection is a strength, not a weakness. Wisdom is born out of this inner struggle for virtue. In the words of Hoyt, "The old failures are to be the scars of growth; the old successes are to be the steps of progress."[40]

Furthermore, it is the author's hope that the descriptions put forth here of a good preacher are general enough to take into consideration the fact that good preachers come in many forms with various strengths and weaknesses. Hoyt offers great insight on this point as well:

> It must be understood that men are called to differing service in the pulpit. To judge all men by the same standards is sheerest folly. One man is an educator, and line upon line patiently instructs people in the essential truth. . . . Another man has the power of bringing knowledge to action. One man has the power to interpret truth. Another man reads the heart and makes its chords to vibrate.[41]

The spiritual, intellectual, social, and physical qualities of preachers are many, but the ones described in this chapter are what the author considers essential to pursue. And God the Knower of all things knows best!

3 On the Craft of Sermon Writing

There is a significant difference between a good sermon and a great sermon. A good sermon is one that features an articulate preacher, offers general wisdom on a loose topic or theme, and inspires a good feeling in the congregation. Such sermons can be delivered extemporaneously by any charismatic preacher. Indeed, the success of such sermons relies largely on the personality and aura of the preacher. A *great* sermon, on the other hand, features a likewise articulate preacher, offers thoughtful and substantial wisdom on a specific topic or theme, and continues to echo in the minds, hearts, and lives of people long after the sermon has concluded. Such sermons can only be delivered with thorough preparation. Indeed, the success of such sermons relies largely on the carefully constructed content of the sermon itself.

This chapter offers advice on preparing a great sermon. Specifically, we will examine the right spiritual and psychological frame of mind with which to approach your sermon preparation, the method of choosing a topic for your sermon, ways of researching your topic, finding the right model for your sermon, developing the four parts of a sermon, five characteristics of a great sermon, and other general advice on the topic.

Approaching the Sermon

The first step in preparing a great sermon is to be in a right spiritual state with God. You can enter this state by performing *wuḍūʾ*, or ritual ablution, and reminding yourself that success only comes through God. Before sitting down to think about your sermon, it is best to soothe your soul with the remembrance of

Allah.[1] This can be done with focused *dhikr* of Allah's Names and *ṣalawāt* upon the Messenger ﷺ, two *rakʿas* of prayer, reciting or listening to the Qur'an, and offering sincere *duʿā'* to Allah to guide you in this task. The most powerful and beautiful *duʿā'* with which a preacher can begin their task is the *duʿā'* that God taught to Moses, upon him be peace, in *sūra Ṭā Hā*, *My Lord! Open my heart, and make my affair easy for me, and loosen the knot from my tongue so that they might fully understand my speech* (Q. 20:25–28; *Rabbi ishraḥ lī ṣadrī, wa-yassir lī amrī, wa-aḥlul ʿuqdatan min lisānī, yafqahū qawlī*). In this marvelous *duʿā'* we find all the elements needed in preparing and delivering a great sermon: spiritual wisdom, Divine aid, and clear, comprehensible speech.

In reality, a good preacher is constantly in a state of "approaching the sermon." In other words, a successful preacher is always seeking out interesting new topics, refreshing illustrations or angles to use in a sermon, and ways to incorporate newfound knowledge or wisdom into the content of a future address. As such, it is useful to keep a small notebook with you wherever you go to write down these thoughts as they come. Sometimes the best ideas will come to you in the middle of the night as you try to fall asleep, so keep this notebook on your bedside as well. As you will see, preparing a great sermon is truly a full-time vocation.

Choosing Your Topic

There are so many topics and themes to preach on, and yet sometimes finding the right topic for the right week can be quite challenging. Generally speaking, there are three options you can consider. The first option is preaching on a general spiritual, ethical, or theological theme that is almost always appealing to a congregation. The second option is preaching on a current event or ongoing situation that is affecting the community. The third option is preaching on a broader social or global issue that is of importance to your congregation and others beyond. All three routes offer good topic destinations, and you will find that different weeks will call for different routes to be taken.

1. Religious Wisdom

These topics can vary in range greatly, but they all carry a common thread of universal appeal such that the topics speak to the human experience beyond time and space. The goal of such sermons is more to remind than to persuade.

According to Hashem's research, this appears to be the most dominant subject addressed in American Friday sermons. Examples of such topics include preferring the afterlife to the temporary abode of this world, being trustworthy, understanding the deeper meanings of monotheism or divine unity (*tawḥīd*), and so on. These topics usually appeal more to the individual than to the communal aspects of life. Since this route has universal appeal, it is a good idea to preach from this route when you find yourself addressing a community with which you are not very familiar. Also, these topics are usually the easiest to preach on because the materials needed to form the content of such sermons are usually readily available within Islam's primary sources. Therefore, if you find yourself with less time to prepare, then this would be an advisable route to follow.

2. Community Issues

This second option gives the preacher an opportunity to address the community of believers as a whole on a topic or theme that has to do with communal behavior or identity. Examples of such topics are etiquettes of disagreement, working together for the common good, and the challenges of raising our youth. The expectation here is that the preacher is at least generally familiar with the community and is aware of the internal and external issues that warrant addressing. A certain level of trust between the preacher and the community is required in order for such sermons to work well. These may not be the easiest topics to broach and will require a careful analysis of the topic you would like to address. Leave enough preparation time to preach on these topics responsibly. When following option two, be careful of preaching only on perceived deficiencies. There are also times when people need positive affirmation and a reminder of the enormous good that is happening. As Hoyt warns preachers, "It is vastly easier to denounce secret sin than to cheer struggling virtue."[2]

My own sense is that American Muslims today are faced with three overarching issues that the American *khaṭīb* is in a prime position to address responsibly: (1) living faithfully in a modern and changing world, (2) a person's religious identity and practice in a minority context, and (3) building a good future for Muslim families and communities in the United States. Preaching on faith and modernity means helping the Muslim community make sense of its moral place in an ever-changing world that is marked by individualism, capitalism, racism, and other similar isms.

An easy and all-too-often employed tactic would be to simply reject modernity altogether and advocate a return to premodernity. We twenty-first-century preachers owe our communities more than that. We can help our communities through these confusing times by carefully reflecting on where Islam stands or ought to stand in relation to some of the isms that have come to define the world we live in today. Modern Muslims are desperate for answers, not just slogans. Our sermons need to offer serious answers to the serious questions posed by modernity. The modern period has also seen a change in the way that people live and interact with innovations—such as mass communication, mass transportation, and instantaneous information (sometimes disinformation and misinformation)—shaping our daily lives. The preacher can offer guidance on how to live as an upright, ethical human being in the midst of all these changes. One of the best sermons that I've heard, for example, focused on proper Islamic etiquettes in our interactions over email and text messages.

Addressing religious identity in a minority context requires instilling confidence in Muslims about their religious beliefs and practices in a culture that is sometimes at odds with the Islamic ethos. The Prophet ﷺ is reported to have said that "Islam began as something strange and it shall return to something strange just as it began; blessedness is for the strangers."[3] When Muslims live in a predominantly non-Muslim society, they are bound to sometimes feel strange in adhering to some Islamic practices. This strangeness is perhaps felt most strongly among youth, who are often asked why they do not date, drink alcohol, or attend school dances. There are also other challenges to being a Muslim minority, such as the constant distorted portrayals of Islam and Muslims in media. All these illustrations are offered to draw attention to the enormous pressures on Muslim identity in the American context. Preachers, then, have an opportunity in their sermons to reassure Muslims about the beauty of their faith, offer advice on the best ways to live as Muslims in America, and challenge the congregation when it needs challenging.

Reflecting on the future of Islam in America, the *khaṭīb* should acknowledge that there is great excitement about the potentials and possibilities ahead but also legitimate anxiety and concerns about what may be around the corner. The American Muslim community is in continual formation, and what shape and direction it will take down the road remains open. What American Muslim culture will look like is still being debated and tested. How Muslims empower themselves in the sociopolitical landscape of America covers a wide range.

All of this is to say that the American Muslim preacher is preaching in a world of possibilities and has opportunities to move the discourse in the right direction and to a higher plane. The American *khaṭīb* can offer a vision of spiritual hope and moral courage that in itself shapes the formation of Islam in the United States.

3. Global Matters

Topics under this third option allow the preacher to preach on something of great importance in the world as a way of addressing a theological or ethical question, mobilizing social action, or both. In the words of Hoyt, "Intellectual and social problems fill the minds of earnest men. . . . The minister is called to be a careful student of such problems."[4] Examples of such topics are confronting the moral problem of poverty, standing up for equity and inclusion, and protecting our planet from climate change. These sermons again require thought and careful research. We tend to preach on these wider social and global issues rarely and almost only when there is a major disaster or catastrophe in the world. As preachers, though, we have a responsibility to focus on these issues, especially when no one else wants to address them. The task here is to inspire moral global citizenship and to make a difference in society. These topics usually have a universal appeal as well and can be preached in many different settings, but the preacher should be careful not to neglect personal and local concerns for wider social and global issues week after week. As stated in chapter 1, remember to "think globally, preach locally."

Regardless of what route you take, the key word in choosing a topic is *relevance.* Only when a topic is presented as relevant will the community of listeners invest in hearing what you have to say. Relevance is determined by how well you can connect your topic to the life experiences and concerns of the congregation. And the only way to connect your topic to people's concerns is to spend time with members of your congregation and to listen to their stories and questions with patience.

When I was a seminary student, the most beneficial task my preaching instructor gave me was to shadow a member of my congregation for one whole day. There is so much that I learned about relevance from that daylong experience. I encourage you to do this with members of your congregation frequently. One warning is offered: when preaching these options, especially two and three, avoid speaking on issues with which you are unfamiliar. Otherwise, misinformation is likely to spread, and you risk delegitimizing yourself in the eyes of your community. Generally speaking, preaching in America means preaching to a very educated, intellectually sophisticated, and literate community. Keep this reality in mind before preaching on any topic, but especially a topic of which you have limited knowledge.

Finding the Right Material

Once you have your sermon topic, you need to find the right material to put together the content of the sermon. The purpose of looking into various sources for your sermon topic is to find material that can support the core teaching, idea, or argument that is being made in your sermon and to find citations that will add illuminating depth to your sermon. The natural place to begin, as always, is with the Qur'an and *Sunna*. There is no better place to ground the legitimacy and authority of your message. Allah Most High says in *sūrat al-ḥujurāt, O you who have attained faith! Do not put yourselves before God and His messenger, but remain conscious of God. Truly God is All-Hearing, All-Knowing* (Q. 49:1). Many commentators have said that this verse means that our teachings, ideas, and arguments should be formulated only after we have examined what the Qur'an and *Sunna* have to say about a specific topic or issue. As a community, Muslims understand this and expect their teachers and preachers to adhere to this etiquette. Many great and successful sermons cite nothing else other than Islam's two primary sources.

The preacher can also draw from the insights, sayings, and teachings of wise companions, scholars, sages, and thinkers from the past fourteen centuries, including our own century. These insights are not compiled in any one place, so this requires much research and study on the part of the preacher. A preacher, then, must read widely.

Lastly, there are less conventional sources to draw on, such as news articles, scientific studies, art, and the like. It is easier to draw on an array of sources if you maintain a thematically organized database of sayings and insights that can be used in future sermons. Maintaining such a record might seem cumbersome, but when you sit down to write your sermons, you will find that it is well worth the time and effort.

When you find supporting and illuminating sources, take care to avoid two common mistakes as you prepare your sermon. The first mistake is to think of these sources, no matter how beautiful and brilliant, as stand-ins for the preacher's own voice and perspective. The congregation has come to hear you, the preacher, not some other source that they can access from the comfort of their own homes. This is not to say that the preacher cannot use a lengthy citation in a sermon every so often, but such invocations need to be broken down into smaller pieces alongside the preacher's own explanation of the referenced text so that the congregation is able to extract the pearls of wisdom found in the lengthy citation. When the preacher simply reads from someone else's work, the congregation can easily become bored and disengage from the sermon.

The second mistake is to expect that words of wisdom found in another language or cultural-historical context will be equally profound for those of another linguistic or cultural background. Non-English sources, including the Qur'an and hadiths, need to be translated with care in order to carry the weight and power that they deserve. There have been many times when I have heard translations of beautiful Qur'anic passages make absolutely no sense because the preacher was careless in the choice of translation. Similarly, if a source uses words, idioms, or illustrations that are alien or perhaps even offensive to the congregation, then all potential benefit will be lost, no matter how much wisdom is contained in the original source. This does not mean that such sources should not be used. Rather, the preacher must go the extra mile in translating not just the exact words but the context as well. To offer an accessible example, when the Prophet ﷺ is quoted as saying, "Wretched are the slaves of the dinar and dirham," the American *khaṭīb* can immediately offer a more contextualized translation: "Wretched are the slaves of dollars and cents."[5]

Choosing the Right Sermon Form

One final step before sitting down to write your sermon is to decide what form you want your sermon to take. By "form" we mean the structure of the sermon. That structure, in turn, is determined by topic, approach, and intention. There are several forms that have developed in Christian preaching that are quite relevant and applicable to the Muslim preaching context. The contemporary scholar of Christian preaching Ronald J. Allen offers a description and analysis of several forms that a sermon can take in his book *Patterns of Preaching: A Sermon Sampler.*[6] Allen notes that sermons have two axes: content and movement. The axis of content can be either expositional or topical. When the content is expositional, the sermon takes a *situation* and interprets it through the lens of scripture. When the content is topical, the sermon takes a *topic* or *theme* and likewise interprets it through the lens of scripture.

As for the axis of movement, a sermon can be either deductive or inductive. A deductive sermon presents a declarative statement or idea at the beginning or near the beginning of the sermon and then uses the rest of the sermon to support its initial claim. Inductive sermons present declarative statements or ideas near the end after starting with a set of questions that are explored through the sermon.

Both forms of movement have their advantages and disadvantages. The advantage of deductive preaching is that it is simple, clear, and direct. Its disadvantage is that it lacks anticipation, since the main point has already been made at the beginning. The advantage of inductive preaching is that it keeps the audience engaged and in anticipation. In fact, the very word *attention* is derived from the idea of being "at tension."[7] The disadvantage is that in the absence of a main point, the audience can lose patience with all the arguments leading up to the main point or declarative statement.[8] You will find that different occasions will call for different movements and that it is best to switch back and forth between these two approaches so that the audience does not become bored with the same form week after week.

Each movement has a set of forms that can be used. Let us begin with approaches found in the deductive sermon that are useful and relevant to Islamic preaching.

1. "Puritan Plain Style"[9]

This form of preaching is direct and to the point. Such a sermon begins with an opening statement or declaration that clearly articulates the central point of the sermon: "My brothers and sisters, prayer is the spiritual practice that keeps us connected to God. It is, in the words of the Prophet ﷺ 'the key to paradise.' And it is the one thing that a Muslim must never let go of no matter what." Of course, such a statement can and should be preceded by a story or illustration that brings the audience into the topic, but it is the statement that sets the course for the rest of the sermon. Then a set of scriptural passages is put forth to support the initial claim. An explanation or interpretation of those passages is offered to further expand upon the initial statement. Before closing, the preacher offers insights into how all of this relates to the life of the congregation. In conclusion, the preacher summarizes their main points and leaves the congregation with food for thought or a call to action. This preaching form is good to use when you want to tackle an issue head-on and, therefore, want to ensure that your message is easily understood. While it might not be the most exciting method for a preacher, there is a reason that it is the oldest and most frequently used.

2. "Sermons That Make Points"[10]

As its name indicates, this form of preaching offers a systematic, point-by-point approach to a particular topic or idea. Once again, the central claim is made at the beginning of a sermon. Then the core substance of the sermon is presented in points, and the sermon concludes with an elucidation of how these points relate to the members of the congregation. The points can either indicate different *aspects* of the central claim or *actions* related to the core teaching. The preacher might begin with something like the following: "Our religion is built on the notion that there is no deity worthy of worship except God. In other words, we believe in absolute monotheism. Today, I would like to focus on three aspects of God's Oneness and how it affects our relationship with God." These are examples of *aspects*-based points. Alternatively, the preacher can begin with something like this: "Our religion is built on the notion that there is no deity worthy of worship except God. In other words, we believe in absolute monotheism. Today, I would like to focus on three ways in which this belief should shape our daily actions and interactions." These are examples of *actions*-based points. The preacher should have these points build upon one another in an interrelated manner. It is best practice to have no more than five points, but ideally three points. The fewer the points, the easier it will be for the congregation to remember them well after the sermon has concluded. This type of sermon is most useful when there are specific teachings or actions that you want the congregation to remember as opposed to a general idea or virtue.

3. "Preaching Verse by Verse"[11]

This form of preaching takes a Qur'anic story or an episode from the life of the Prophet Muhammad ﷺ and uses it to expound on a topic or idea that is of relevance to the congregation. The main point is drawn from the narratives of scripture themselves. This sermon form usually begins with placing the chosen story in its historical and scriptural context and then methodically recounting the story. The story is told not as a matter of dry repetition, but it ought to be told in a way that is constantly shifting between the world of scripture and our own. The sermon is concluded with the major lessons or core teaching that the sermon intends to draw from the chosen story. This form of preaching is very useful when there is a clear analogy between a current situation and a scriptural situation.

4. "Thesis-Antithesis-Synthesis"[12]

This form of preaching has three components: thesis, antithesis, and synthesis. A thesis is an observation about the way a particular ethical or theological issue is understood. An antithesis is an exposition on the flaws found in the thesis. A synthesis is an attempt to explain the ethical or theological issue anew, mediating between thesis and antithesis. Such sermons are particularly useful in teaching-preaching when the preacher wants to correct or clarify a commonly held incorrect religious view.

5. "Contrasting Perspectives"[13]

This form of preaching offers two different perspectives on a particular moral or theological issue. Each perspective is thoroughly and fairly examined and articulated. The distinctiveness of these two positions is honored and celebrated, and there is no attempt at synthesis. An appropriate conclusion would be to offer insight into how these two perspectives can coexist within the same community. Such sermons are most effective when the community is split on a particular issue that really does have two or more valid positions. The preacher can help play the role of mediator by engaging in this preaching form.

Having covered these major approaches to inductive preaching, let us turn our attention now to the models best suited for inductive preaching that would be of benefit to Muslim preachers. I have identified three, which include the following:

6. "Simple Inductive Preaching"[14]

The chief characteristic of inductive preaching is that it "creates tension" and unfolds as an "experience of discovery."[15] The sermon opens with a set of questions or unresolved issues usually stemming from a situation or experience. Materials are then gathered one by one from various sources, ranging from scripture to the arts, that seek to resolve the tension that has been created in the opening. This type of preaching is most useful when the topic at hand really is a question that is in the hearts and minds of the audience or when the preacher wants to propose an idea that is new or an idea with which the audience may even initially disagree. By posing your idea as a question, you invite the audience to explore the issue with you, which in turn allows for more difficult or challenging issues to be addressed.

7. "Preaching from Oops to Yeah"[16]

This form of preaching continues to exploit the creative tension that is inherent in inductive preaching. The sermon begins by introducing a problem and ends with a solution to that problem. In other words, "The sermon begins with an itch. The sermon seeks to scratch the itch."[17] Eugene Lowry, who describes this form of sermon, writes that there are "five moments" involved.[18] First is the moment of "Oops," in which the problem is introduced. The problem is a doubt or challenge that rises out of Islamic scripture, theology, or practice. The second moment is known as "Ugh," in which the preacher further reflects on why the problem is a problem. The third moment is known as "Aha," where "a sudden shift appears" and a hint is given of the answer to the problem.[19] Then from this emerges the moment of "Whee," where the preacher nurtures the hint into a full-grown convincing answer. The fifth and final moment is "Yeah," in which the preacher reflects on how this newfound answer can shape the future. This preaching form works best when there is genuine concern or doubt about an aspect of faith that the congregation needs help resolving.

8. "Topical Preaching"[20]

This form of preaching allows the preacher to explore with the congregation the deeper meaning of ideas or concepts found in the Islamic ethos. Such a sermon usually begins with introducing the topic and explaining why it is important to reflect on. Then, the preacher gathers sources from the tradition to delve into the various meanings and aspects of the topic. This sermon form concludes with how this understanding of the topic can shape the life of the congregation. Here too the sermon begins with the creative tension of a question, but the uncovering of its answer is more direct and scripture-centric. An example of this would be exploring all the different contexts in which the Qur'an and hadiths use the concept of *jihād* as a way of explaining its multifaceted nature and scope. This preaching method can be used when the preacher feels that expounding upon a particular Islamic concept would be helpful in the spiritual or ethical life of a congregation.

The Four Parts of a Sermon

A great sermon is a memorable sermon. A sermon that rings true in the hearts and minds of listeners well after it has been delivered is the greatest measure of successful preaching. There are four parts to any sermon: (1) an opening that draws in the audience; (2) the main body, in which excellent rhetoric and illustrations are used to develop the core idea or teaching; (3) a conclusion that drives home the message; and (4) a closing prayer that offers a way forward. For an address to be memorable, all four parts need to be written well with an eye toward delivering a beautiful sermon.

1. The Opening

Studies have shown that the average attention span of people today is incredibly short—about thirty seconds. Therefore, the opening of the sermon is of vital importance. The congregation comes to the site of the sermon with a list of errands and concerns on their mind. Within the first thirty seconds or so, many in the audience will determine whether the sermon is worth their time. A successful opening will help transition the audience's attention away from their busy lives to the life of the sermon.

It is a blessing that our Islamic sermons must always begin with invocations that precede the substance of our sermon. When these invocations are articulated with a strong, confident, and beautiful voice, the listeners are able to transition into a spiritual mindfulness that facilitates proper hearing and understanding. Then the preacher has the opportunity to bring the audience fully into the sermon with a compelling opening statement, question, or story. Stories, when told well, can capture the congregation's attention and imagination. Consider the following two ways that a sermon about preparing for death and the afterlife can begin:

> My brothers and sisters, as we know, the life of this world is temporary and quickly fleeting. It is from wisdom and intelligence, then, that we prepare every day for that moment of death which every human being is guaranteed to experience and for what comes after it.

Here, the strategy of using an opening statement is used to engage the audience. Alternatively, one might begin with an anecdote:

> My dear brothers and sisters, I want to tell you the story of a young man by the name of Yahya ibn Salih. Yahya was a university student who was full of life, a brilliant student, and an active member of the local Muslim community on campus. One day, a few weeks before Ramadan, Yahya was engaged in one of those long board meetings in which all the logistics for the upcoming holy month were being planned. Toward the end of this meeting, one of the members of the board raised the issue of what would happen were someone to pass away in the community given that there were no Islamic burial services or graveyards in the area. Yahya, needing to return to his studies, jokingly said, "I have a long life ahead of me, why don't you old-timers discuss this issue among yourselves." Everyone on the board laughed and bid Yahya farewell. Nearly an hour later, a panicked call came to the masjid—Yahya had been in a terrible car crash. The members of the board quickly got into their cars and drove to the hospital. Upon arriving, Yahya's friends were given the shocking news. Yahya ibn Salih, may Allah rest his soul, returned to his Lord at the age of twenty. From Allah we come and to Him is our return. Life is a blessing, and its continuation is guaranteed to no one. How, then, do we prepare for that moment of death and for what is to come after it?

In this version, the use of a story joined to a question is deployed to engage the audience. Arguably, this strategy makes for a more appealing opening than that of the plain statement.

There are three tips to keep in mind when pondering the opening phase of your sermon. First, the opener should be a natural introduction to the rest of the content of the sermon. While stories are most effective as openers, it is wiser to use appealing statements or questions if you are unable to find a story that perfectly flows into your sermon. A story that is disjointed from the rest of the sermon is ineffective. Second, the opening should be relatively brief and to the point. A rule of thumb is that your opening should not be longer than three minutes. The congregation is eager to know what your topic is and will lose patience if this phase stretches on for too long. Third (and we will discuss this more in the following chapter), the opening statement, question, or story must be something that you can either memorize or recall fairly accurately in your own words in an articulate and free-flowing manner. The opener is an opportunity for the preacher to establish a connection between themselves and the audience. That connection is made when the preacher presents the opener looking into the eyes of people in the audience rather than at a piece of paper.

Finally, a note of caution about the opener. Never begin with an apology or an excuse. I have been surprised to see how many times our Muslim preachers begin by saying that they truly do not deserve to be speaking or that they did not have enough time to prepare properly. The preacher may have intended to convey humility and honesty, but what the audience is likely to hear is, "This is not going to be worth your time." As a result, the audience is likely to disengage. Humility can be conveyed in many ways without turning the audience off. For example, "I am truly humbled to be standing here before you." An apology for unpreparedness, however, is unacceptable. Even if you are asked to preach at the last minute, as is too often the case in many communities, either focus on sharing something useful or do not accept the invitation to the pulpit or podium at all.

2. The Main Body

The structure of the main body will depend on the form of the sermon with which you choose to go. The main body is where your core teaching or idea will be presented to the congregation. The preacher may use many ways to say the same thing or convey the same point. What great preachers learn to do is to articulate their message using the clearest, most appropriate, most effective, and most memorable language possible. One of the descriptions that we have of the Prophet ﷺ is that his speech was always easy to understand, concise in its length, and effective in its reception. With regard to clear language, clarity means using short sentences and concise words to make your point. It also means using words that everyone can understand without having to open a dictionary.

Concerning appropriateness, preaching with the most appropriate language means using words that best convey the message and facilitate understanding without erecting barriers. For example, when the preacher translates *ʿibād Allāh* as "slaves of Allah," they might inadvertently erect a barrier in the minds and hearts of listeners who associate slavery with the most heinous of oppressions and are unable to hear "slave" in a positive context. As such, using a term like "servants of Allah" facilitates understanding without raising an unexpected cause for concern and can be considered more appropriate even if slightly less accurate. Of course, an ability to read the context of the community here matters greatly. A preacher is more likely to be in tune with what is and is not appropriate language if they are intimately familiar with the culture and history of the congregation.

Regarding efficacy, using the most effective language means employing words that are most likely to have the intended effect on the community of listeners. Particular words inspire, warn, and delight more than others. Finding those key words that help foster the intended mood makes the sermon that much more powerful. For example, words such as *compassion* and *love* stir the softer qualities of our human nature. Words such as *justice* and *courage* evoke stronger qualities.

Memorable language is best achieved through illustrations. Illustrations are words and sentences that inspire images and feelings in the minds and hearts of a congregation. Illustrations work as visual aids to the spoken word. Successful evocations, then, transfer the preacher's teachings into the more enduring compartments of human memory and consciousness. Successful illustrations also bridge gaps of understanding so that difficult or unfamiliar concepts may be more easily understood. But what makes a good illustration? To help answer that question, I will draw heavily upon the writings of Webb Garrison, a scholar of Christian preaching, in his book *The Preacher and His Audience.* Illustrations primarily take the form of what are known as "figures of speech." There are several figures of speech at the preacher's disposal, so it is worth knowing them all and using them wisely.

Alliteration.[21] Alliteration "exploits the sounds of words"[22] by repeating the first letters of words in a sequence of two or more words. Alliteration can be especially useful if you want to join a larger idea with a memorable term. For example, a preacher can say, "The grand project before us, my brothers and sisters, is to create compassionate communities in every county of this country." "Create compassionate communities" is a catchy phrase that the audience is likely to remember and that can, in the future, be used as a motto for a movement that springs out of this idea. Moreover, "county of this country" further creates a sense of harmony between the ideas in the sentence. It is best to reserve alliterations for special occasions when you want to convey an idea rather than simply beautify your rhetoric.

Onomatopoeia.[23] Similar to alliteration, onomatopoeia is a rhetorical device that plays on the sounds of words by using words that in themselves convey meaning. A good example of this in Arabic is the word *waswasa*, or "whisper," which through its very vocalization conveys such a meaning. Onomatopoeia is helpful in stressing particular terms or in creating an intended mood in the audience. For instance, the preacher can say in a hushed tone, "Do not be deluded away from the truth by the *waswasa* of *Shayṭān*" with a powerful effect.

Metaphor and Simile.[24] A metaphor is an analogy that the preacher offers to explain an idea or concept. Metaphors are especially useful in explaining something that the audience might find difficult to grasp. They are gifts that keep on giving. This is perhaps the greatest tool that a preacher has in their possession. Metaphors are used frequently in Qur'anic and prophetic preaching. For example, the Qur'an likens the evil of backbiting to *eating the dead flesh of your brother* (Q. 49:12). Similarly, the Prophet ﷺ relates in a well-known *ḥadīth qudsī* that God says, "And if he comes to Me walking, I come to him running."[25]

Akin to metaphor is simile. The difference is technical. In metaphor, a comparison is used without indicating that it is just a comparison, expecting that the audience will realize the intention. The simile is an analogy that uses the word *like* to precede the comparison. A preacher, then, who is preaching on the concept of *zuhd*, or nonattachment to the things of this world, might say, "Be a traveler in the journey of this life," or "Be *like* a traveler in the journey of this life." There is no clear advantage or disadvantage to the use of either metaphor or simile in drawing analogies, but it does seem, from this author's limited knowledge, that Qur'anic and prophetic preaching use simile more than metaphor as a figure of speech.

Allegory.[26] An allegory is a lengthier metaphor that typically takes the form of an imaginative story. Allegory can be useful when the preacher wants to draw attention to a type of person or phenomenon, whether good or bad, without specifying who or what the story is referring to today. An allegory is an extended metaphor of an imaginary, but potentially real, person or incident. The sister of allegory is fable. Fables are even longer metaphors made up of imaginary characters doing imaginary things. The most common fables are analogies made between human beings and animals. A story that presents something like "The lion then said to the mouse" would be considered a fable. Allegories are commonly used in the instructional tales of the Sufis.

Parable.[27] While like allegories and fables, parables do not seek to make a one-to-one analogy. Rather, a parable offers just "one important point of resemblance."[28] For example, a preacher preaching on the ills of displaying anger in the home might say, "Parents who do not learn to manage their anger early on are like parents who bring home a baby lion for the children to play with. Slowly, that lovable pet will grow into a terrifying beast!" This would be considered a parable as opposed to an allegory or fable since it is focused on just one aspect of the analogy.

Personification.[29] Personification gives other creatures or inanimate subjects humanlike qualities. Personification is useful in engaging the audience's creative capacity to imagine things that are beyond the perception of this earthly life. A powerful use of this device is found in *sūrat al-zalzala*, *When the earth is shaken to her utmost convulsion, and when the earth releases her burdens, and the human being cries out, "What has happened to her?" On that Day she will recall all her chronicles* (Q. 99:1–4).

Hyperbole.[30] A hyperbole is used to convey a major incident or thing in an exaggerated manner without broaching the absurd. The exaggeration is not necessarily false. Its intent, rather, is to magnify the point being made. For example, this is found when the Qur'an speaks of God's all-knowing attribute in *sūrat al-an'ām*, *Not a leaf falls without Him knowing it* (Q. 6:59). Hyperbole is an especially useful figure of speech when the preacher is speaking about Allah the Majestic.

Irony.[31] Irony is a form of humor in which the preacher says the opposite of what they really mean. Irony or satire can be easily misunderstood by the audience and can even take away from the good message of the preacher. So when it is used, it should be used very carefully.

Rhetorical Questions.[32] The posing of rhetorical questions is very effective and used commonly in Qur'anic and prophetic preaching. A question is asked with the intention of prompting the audience to think and reflect rather than answer immediately. Rhetorical questions engage the audience and make them feel as if they are part of an ongoing conversation. Rhetorical questions can also be a powerful way to conclude a sermon and drive home a point. I remember one of the most effective sermons that had a lasting impact on my life concluded by asking in a very powerful and eloquent way, "What have you done to prepare for that Day?"—the last day—three times.

Proverbs. Proverbs are well-known sayings found within a particular culture or tradition, such as "No pain, no gain" or "Turn the other cheek." They are cultural touchstones with which a community is conversant and familiar. In Muslim cultural settings, many hadiths function like cultural proverbs, such as "Even a smile is charity." By associating your message with a proverb, your message becomes more identifiable and, thus, more memorable. In effect, you can refamiliarize your audience with an old and known saying, possibly even disclosing to them a new appreciation for it.

Persuasion toward a Decision.[33] This means illustrating for your audience two conceivable yet distinct paths in life, typically good versus evil. The Qur'an uses this rhetorical device quite powerfully in *sūrat al-balad* when Allah speaks of two highways, one leading toward a good end and the other toward a bad one (Q. 90:10–20). The preacher can offer powerful sermons distinguishing in detail the path of God versus the path of Satan, or the path of worldliness versus the path of otherworldliness, or similar.

Additionally, there are some key characteristics of good illustrations that are important to keep in mind as you develop your own illustrations in your sermons. First, good illustrations are always interesting. An interesting illustration is one that engages the mind and inspires the heart. Simply put, such an illustration is relevant by speaking to the concerns and context of your congregation.[34] Be sure that your illustration matches the quality of your sermon. Do not offer a childish illustration on a serious topic, for example.[35] Be careful with using the same illustration frequently; your congregation will grow tired of it rather quickly even if it is a good one. Second, good illustrations are always instructive. Instructive illustrations are easily understood and support the main point of the sermon.[36] As a rule of thumb, an illustration that requires an explanation is a bad illustration. Illustrations are there to explain, not to be explained. Third, good illustrations should be persuasive. Persuasive illustrations are ones that make sense and ring true to the listeners.[37] Know your congregation well before formulating an illustration.

Not all illustrations are equally persuasive in every setting or across different segments of people. There is nothing worse than erroneous and false illustrations. Such illustrations are not only useless but also counterproductive, and they render the preacher and their message as unreliable. Moreover, beware of the temptation to personalize a story that you received secondhand. Not only does such a deception violate even the most basic ethical standards to which a preacher is expected to adhere, but if the truth were ever to be revealed, the harm done to your credibility would be irreparable.[38]

3. The Conclusion

Now that we have talked about what a good introduction looks like and how to use language and illustrations in writing the main body of your sermon, we turn our attention to the conclusion of the sermon. A conclusion is the preacher's final chance to drive home their message and to inspire the intended effect. A conclusion is also the last thing that an audience will hear and, therefore, will be most likely to remember. As such, it is essential that serious time and attention be spent on crafting a good conclusion. A good conclusion has three major characteristics: (1) it offers a take-home message, (2) it inspires a particular action or behavior, and (3) it leaves the audience wanting more.

A *take-home message* can take the form of a final illustration, such as a story, poem, or summary statement that sums up the major points of a sermon. If you use an illustration, be sure that it is fully connected to the central point of the sermon and that it does not introduce new or additional issues or questions. The point of a conclusion is to close the lid on the can, not to open a whole new can of worms. If you conclude using summary points, then articulate those points using some of the rhetorical devices discussed in the previous section to make your points interesting and memorable.

By *inspiring a particular action or behavior*, the sermon fulfills its most important task. People are usually inspired to do something when their feelings and emotions have been touched. As such, a good conclusion must have that emotional touch to it. Intellectual appeals can be left primarily for the main body, where core arguments are formulated in the sermon. It would be wise for the preacher to coordinate beforehand with institutional managers to see if the virtue preached in the sermon can be immediately implemented. An easy example is if a preacher preaches on the virtue of charity, then it would be a great opportunity for there to be a particular charitable cause to which people can donate as they leave.

A conclusion that *leaves the audience wanting more* is a truly successful conclusion. Ibn al-Jawzī reports about one of the earliest preachers in Islamic history, ʿAbd Allāh b. Masʿūd (d. 32/652–3), that "he would discourse to us and then suddenly stop while our interest was still running high and we were wishing that he would continue."[39] In other words, a good conclusion will leave the congregation reflecting and pondering over the central teaching or idea both individually and collectively.

4. The Closing Prayer

Like the opening, an Islamic sermon will always end with a *duʿāʾ*, or supplicatory prayer. This prayer helps the audience transition from the life of the sermon back to the life of this world. Therefore, a prayer should be optimistic and forward-looking as it seeks to deliver its audience back to the safe shores of the earth after riding a high wave of enthusiasm. Certain standard invocations fit with any sermon and should not be neglected, but it is a good idea to begin these invocations with your own special prayer that relates to the sermon's main point. If the topic of your sermon is courage, for instance, you can begin your closing prayer with words like these: "O Allah, we ask You by Your immense bounty to make our hearts firm upon this religion, to give us the courage to always seek the truth wherever it may lie, and to do good even when it is difficult, unpopular, or criticized. O Allah, let our courage spring from our love of pleasing You and our love of gaining Your blessings and from a fear of being distant from You or Your blessings for even the blink of an eye." In this way, the final phase of the sermon is connected to its other more substantial parts, and what you have, God willing, in the end are the makings of a great sermon—a sermon made to be remembered.

Five Characteristics of a Great Sermon

Once you have written the first draft of your sermon, you need to go back and revise it. As you begin the revision process, it is important to have a clear idea of what a great sermon looks and feels like. Here are five characteristics of a great sermon, in no particular order, that will help you assess whether your sermon is ready for delivery.

1. Brief, Organized, and to the Point

One quality of a great sermon is that it is relatively brief, well-organized, and to the point. Today, the spoken word, no matter how great, has a difficult time competing with the relentless draw exerted by our consumer culture societies. The attention span of the average listener is at an all-time low, according to researchers. Therefore, if we want our sermons to be memorable, we must learn to preach effectively in a short amount of time. Furthermore, in our American Muslim context, preachers should be sensitive to the fact that most members of the congregation need to return immediately to work or classes. It would be wise for preachers to take seriously the prophetic counsel, "The length of a man's prayer and the shortness of his oration are a sign of his understanding [the religion]. So, make the prayer long and the oration short."[40] When we look at the recorded sermons of the Prophet ﷺ, they are usually only a few paragraphs long and can be read slowly and methodically in less than ten minutes. Likewise, the great jurist Aḥmad b. Ḥanbal (d. 241/855) is reported to have said, "I do not like to see a *qāṣṣ* [preacher] boring the people. When he exhorts the people he should not permit the meeting to drag on."[41] In a similar vein, al-Zuhrī (d. 232/846) states, "When the meeting draws out Satan will profit from it."[42]

The more you prepare and hone your message, the more you will find that it is easier to be concise. One mistake that many preachers make is to think that everything that needs to be said on a given topic must be said in one sermon. This is far from true. In fact, focusing on just one aspect of a topic is much more effective than covering all aspects at once. Other opportunities, God willing, will arise to build on the same topic in future sermons. Opinions vary, but twenty-five minutes seems to be the maximum amount of time an average listener is going to remain attentive. Plan on spending no more than fifteen minutes on the first part of your *khuṭba* and no more than ten minutes on the second part. The interval between the two parts of the *khuṭba* should be used to regain the focus and attention of your congregation.

2. Balanced

A second quality that you should look for in your sermon is balance. Balance means that the content of your sermon should maintain a middle path between extremes. For example, many of our sermons are too pessimistic in content and reprimanding in tone. Centuries ago, Ibn al-Jawzī complained of extreme preachers who caused people to abandon life altogether, saying, "If the *qāṣṣ* [preacher] possessed understanding he would have informed his hearers that what is to be censured are the excesses of this world which distract from the hereafter, but that material things in and of themselves are a necessity."[43] Ibn al-Jawzī goes on to warn against extremist preaching, especially in difficult or sensitive times:

> Some of them [the preachers] mention death, the separation of death (*firāq*), and the ruination of decrepitude. They repeatedly mention these calamities to the women and to the weak in heart, and they cause them to resent the decrees of God. These topics constitute the major part of what they say in the ceremonies of condolence (*aʿzīya*), this being among the abominable things. It is proper and fitting only that the people who suffer misfortune be commanded to patiently endure their misfortune, but in point of fact they are goaded on to [even greater] anxiety.[44]

The Messenger ﷺ taught us to "make things easy and do not make them difficult, cheer the people up by conveying glad tidings to them and do not repulse (them)."[45] As such, a great sermon will appeal to both the intellect and the emotions, inspire both hope and awe, stress goodness in both the vertical relationship with God and the horizontal relationship with fellow beings, and so on. This balance can be difficult to achieve in a sermon, and it is unlikely that there will be complete balance, but at least some semblance of it ought to be sought.

3. Reads Well Aloud

A third quality to keep in mind as you read your sermon is to hear whether it reads well aloud. In other words, the written form and the spoken form are quite different. You must write your sermon with an eye toward delivering it. Something can look truly beautiful in words but come off as rather dull or strained when preached. As a rule of thumb, when you read your sermon, you yourself should feel inspired by it and should feel the same effects as you intend for your congregation. Remember, only an inspired preacher can inspire. Along the same lines, a great sermon will purposefully plant rhetorical devices throughout that are aimed at maintaining or returning people's attention to the sermon. As Garrison writes, "It is a fallacy to think of attention as a single total response to a sermon. Attention must be captured, held, and recaptured many times in twenty-five minutes."[46] The success of this might be difficult to gauge when you are reading your own sermon, so take the advice of an honest friend, such as your spouse, to determine if there are enough attention-grabbing moments in the address.

4. Relevant

A fourth quality of your sermon should be that it is completely relevant to the listeners and that every aspect of your message is in harmony with the reality of people's lives. Relevance, of course, begins with the topic that you choose, but it extends to the words you employ, the analogies you offer, and the deeds you encourage. As you write and revise your *khuṭba*, think of three or four regular members of your congregation, and ask yourself if the *khuṭba* you are preparing is indeed relevant to their lives and in harmony with their realities.

5. Inclusive

A fifth and essential quality of a great sermon is that the language of the sermon is inclusive of the audience for which it is intended. Is everyone made to feel that they are addressed in that moment together? Inclusivity begins with the language we use. One very common mistake that preachers make is to preach as if there are no women present in the audience. To say things like "My dear brothers," to translate *insān* as "man" or "mankind" instead of "human being" or "humankind," to use only "he" in an analogy or story, or to only tell stories of great men of faith and never the stories of great women of faith is to exclude and alienate part of the congregation. At the very least, the preacher should avoid divisiveness and exclusion in their address. Garrison reflects on this aspect brilliantly:

> Anything that tends to set any listener apart as a spectator and outsider rather than as a participant should be scrupulously avoided. Consider the typical announcement: "*We* are glad to have *you visitors* with *us* today. *We* welcome you back to worship with *us* at any time." While this statement may be made with the best of intentions, it tends to emphasize the visitor's awareness that he does not belong to the "we group." . . . Every possible effort should be exerted to create a "we" relationship between the speaker and every member of the larger conversational group that is the preaching situation.[47]

At another level, the preacher can do things, especially useful at the outset, to unite the congregation in the experience of the sermon. For example, beginning with a set of "we" statements can achieve this goal. The use of "we" could look something like this: "We begin by praising Allah, the Creator and Sustainer of the universe; we praise Allah for His mercy, compassion, kindness, generosity, love, and forgiveness; we thank Allah for bringing us together and uniting our hearts in His remembrance; and, we bear witness with full clarity on our tongues and conviction in our hearts that there is no deity worthy of worship except Allah and that Muhammad (sws) is indeed His servant and final messenger." There are also rhetorical devices that can unite the congregation. For example, careful use of humor can bind people together in the common experience of laughter.

On the Timeline and Other Final Thoughts

The prescription for preparing a great sermon might seem quite daunting at first, but after practice, the process promises to become easier and quicker over time.

Nevertheless, ease and speed are not our primary aims. In fact, if anything, this chapter encourages Islamic preachers to think hard, to put time and sufficient preparation into their vocation, and to discourage the current culture of preaching off the cuff. Honestly speaking, many poorly prepared and delivered sermons could become good with just a little bit of effort, and many decent or good sermons could become great with some extra effort. As a rule of thumb, if you spend less than an hour preparing for your address, then you are most likely ill-prepared. Ideally, no less than two hours should be spent preparing and practicing a *khuṭba*. A proposed timeline might be helpful here, although each preacher will eventually find a process that works best for them. Those weeks when I am organized, I take some time on Saturday to think of a good and relevant topic. On Sunday, that topic is finalized and narrowed in its scope to a single focus. On Monday, I begin researching material for the *khuṭba* and determining the right sermon form for the topic. Tuesday and Wednesday are spent writing and rewriting the sermon until it reaches its final form. On Thursday, I practice giving the address several times over and try to memorize enough of it to preach from an outline written on note cards. On Friday morning, final preparations are made for preaching in the afternoon.

In conclusion, we must always remember and realize that the Islamic preacher is blessed with a beautiful religion that really has the capacity, in many ways, to speak for itself through the wisdom of the Qur'an and prophetic example. The opportunity of putting together a beautiful sermon that reminds, teaches, and inspires the community is a delightful blessing and a cause for joy. There is wisdom in showing and expressing constant gratitude to God for giving us the strength to preach and granting us the great company of those who call people to God and goodness. When the task of preaching is performed with this spirit, God facilitates and eases the process.

And success only comes through Allah the Sublime.

4 On the Delivery of the Sermon

THE ART OF PREACHING ACHIEVES REALIZATION when a thoughtfully crafted sermon is delivered as an experience that engages, inspires, and illuminates an audience. Essentially, great words of wisdom and insight are neatly etched into the permanent memory and consciousness of listeners through the preaching experience. The message delivered, therefore, is not only moving but also deeply meaningful. A sermon delivered with such power can best be referred to as an "effective sermon." This chapter will focus on the tools needed to deliver an effective sermon. Specifically, we will discuss the ways to foster the right mood, prepare for a great delivery, command the audience's attention, orchestrate the intended effects, overcome obstacles, maintain the proper etiquette of the pulpit, and develop a sound process to evaluate and improve upon one's preaching.

Preparing to Preach with Spiritual Confidence

As much time as preachers put into writing a sermon, the success of a sermon will depend ultimately on how well it is delivered. That success depends, in part, on the spiritual and psychological state of the preacher, which is marked by an aura of confidence. This confidence is not the attitude one gains from overestimating oneself; rather, it is the disposition one gains from the calmness that God instills into the heart of a servant. The inward state of a preacher gives preaching its real power and beauty. At the same time, outward preparation affects inward reality. Ibn al-Jawzī quotes an anonymous scholar as saying, "If a man's appearance does not profit you, neither will his exhortations."[1]

On the day of preaching, be sure to eat a small yet healthy breakfast. This meal should be enough to give you energy for the physically exhausting task of preaching but not so much as to weigh you down on the pulpit. Avoid consuming foods with excessive spice, acidity, and other potential discomforts. To stay hydrated, drink plenty of water or a rehydrating sports drink. Refresh your senses with a good bath and nice-smelling musk, as was the practice of the Prophet ﷺ on Fridays, which in Arabic is called the day of *jumuʿa* or "gathering."

Be sure to groom yourself well, but without extravagance, so that your appearance on the pulpit facilitates listening and is not a cause for distraction. Keep mints on hand so that the fragrance of your breath is pleasing rather than repulsive. Cough drops or lozenges offer an added benefit in maintaining the strength of your voice throughout the sermon. Be sure to dress well and appropriately, as the Prophet Muhammad ﷺ said, "Allah loves to see the marks of His Bounties on his servant."[2] A long, simple, modest shirt with full sleeves is preferable for the occasion of preaching as well. As recorded by al-Nawawī, the sleeves of the Prophet's *qamīṣ*, or shirt, "reached down to his wrists."[3] Again, your dress should facilitate listening rather than distraction. Avoid unsecured cloaks and similar dress that might fall from the shoulders, as it will distract you from the duty of preaching and may well distract your audience as well. All these matters may seem of little importance, but our visual senses so often overpower our auditory ones. Therefore, appearances are of utmost importance in creating a successful preaching experience. Too many preachers undervalue their outward appearance to their own detriment. I once attended a *khuṭba* in which the *khaṭīb* was wearing a Hawaiian shirt with colorful palm trees. Obviously, the only thing I remember from that *khuṭba* is the Hawaiian shirt. Alkhairo offers additional insight into the importance of dressing right for the occasion of preaching:

> Looking your best on the *minbar* adds to your credibility in the eyes of the audience. A well-groomed speaker gives the impression that he takes the occasion seriously. His appearance reflects on his organization and confidence. Attention should also be paid to clothing, its colors and patterns. Bright colors or large patterns can have a dazzling and distracting effect on the listener.[4]

All this outward preparation would be considered superficial if it came at the cost of neglecting the inward state of the preacher when standing on the pulpit.

Put another way, a preacher cannot inspire if not inspired, cannot remind if not reminded, and cannot transform if not transformed.

On the day of preaching, take the time needed to center yourself so that you may be solely with your Lord. Offer a sincere *duʿāʾ* or supplication beginning with the *duʿāʾ* of the Prophet Moses, peace be upon him. Recite and reflect on *sūrat al-kahf* (Q. 18) following the prophetic Friday practice for the time leading up to the congregational prayer. On the drive or walk to the site of preaching, recite continuously the attributes and praises of Allah Most High. Then upon entering the site, greet people with words of peace and with a spirit of humility and good cheer. Turn to the *qibla*, the direction of prayer, and offer the number of *rakʿa* due to a place of worship (*taḥiyyat al-masjid*) according to your *madhab*, or school of law.

After completing your prayers, walk over to the pulpit using gentle steps and without stepping over anyone, and turn to your congregation and offer the best and most complete greetings of peace in a slow, clear manner, preferably with a smile. As the *adhān*, or call to prayer, is called out to precede your sermon, sit still in reverence of what is being chanted and repeat each line of the *adhān* in your heart and quietly on your tongue. Before standing to begin your *khuṭba*, offer a short supplication asking for Allah's grace and help to aid in your preaching. All this advice is from none other than the *Sunna* of the Beloved of Allah ﷺ, and what a beautiful model we have in the Messenger of God ﷺ.

The beauty of one's inward state has an opportunity to expand once more through the sincere voicing of God's praise, the testimony of faith, and other invocations that precede the main content of the sermon. At the end of the first part of the *khuṭba*, there is another spiritually renewing moment in which the *khaṭīb* asks the congregation to repent before sitting down to ask for personal forgiveness as well. Finally, at the conclusion of the *khuṭba*, there is a chance for heartfelt *duʿāʾ* to be made as the *khaṭīb* transitions into leading the prayer. All of this is to say that God, through the model of the Prophet ﷺ, has given the preacher all the opportunities needed to preach with a towering soul and a soft heart. Using these methods, the preacher can attain the highest spiritual confidence needed to preach a great sermon.

Turning the Written Word into Spoken Art

Once you have completed the difficult task of writing a great sermon, there are three ways to convert your drafted sermon into a form that is ready for preaching.

The first method is to take your manuscript with you up to the pulpit in its entirety and to preach directly from it. It is less than ideal for a good, let alone a great, preacher to read the sermon from a piece of paper or screen. This type of delivery can be dull, disconnected, and disengaging. Rather, what we mean by preaching from the full text is that the preacher has committed the sermon to memory, or is at least thoroughly familiar with it, so as to be able to preach directly to the audience while only glancing occasionally at the text as an aid or as a reference for citations. The advantage of preaching from the full text is that you have the entire text with you if perchance you forget or stumble. Moreover, it is also easier to remind yourself of what is coming up next as you conclude a major point. The disadvantage of this method is that an inexperienced preacher, upon the first sign of trouble, might begin reading the written sermon word for word rather than preaching from it. There is a temptation to rely too heavily on the paper or screen in front of us when using this method.

If you do choose to go with preaching from the written word, which is a common preference, then keep the following points in mind. When it comes to a printed sermon, aim for visual clarity at a distance when selecting font, and be sure to choose a sufficiently legible font size. The same holds true for line spacing. Once printed, consider annotating the right-hand margin with just three words or less on what each major paragraph is about to help you transition from one part to the next. You can use the left-hand margin in a similar way to signal gestures you might want to use at different points. Remember that the delivery of the sermon is an embodied practice. Lastly, avoid folding, rolling, or curling your printed sermon by carrying it in a folder or the like. A malformed manuscript is likely to fold over or even fall off a podium while you preach.

Much of this advice remains true with respect to digital screens. Whether using a laptop, tablet, smartphone, or another electronic device, keep legibility at the foremost of your mind. Be mindful of potentially losing your place if the document you are viewing jumps ahead due to an oversensitive touchscreen or trackpad. Turn off notifications and close unnecessary apps and programs. Adjust the settings to ensure that the screen remains on throughout your delivery. Finally, if you have the opportunity, gauge the space where you will be standing to deliver the sermon. Does it provide a surface capable of supporting your device or its stand? While electronic devices may possess a certain convenience, think too of how your delivery might be perceived as you read from a screen.

Some preachers find the presence of a completely written sermon to be too distracting or too constraining, making the whole preaching experience stale and unauthentic. For such a preacher, a less distracting method is to make a thorough outline of the prepared sermon and to preach from the outline instead. In this method too, the preacher is expected to commit the sermon to memory or at least be intimately familiar with it. The burden of exactitude, however, is significantly less. Obviously, certain lines or points are only effective if they are spoken precisely; such sentences can be included in full in the outline. The advantage of such a method is that the preacher is more likely to employ an informal style of preaching rather than a more rigid, formal style. This method also wards off the temptation to read while providing enough material to stay on message should one's rhythm be momentarily lost. The disadvantage is that the outline does not provide enough of a safety net should the preacher be overcome with anxiety. At the end of the day, an outline is still a prepared document that is potentially distracting to the preacher and audience. As such, many preachers have started off their vocation with the first method and slowly transitioned to the second as they became more confident in their role at the pulpit.

If you choose this second method, then keep the following points in mind. A thorough outline will be organized according to each core part of the sermon. These parts will be expressed by a main title that indicates the topic and a subtitle that says more about the main topic. Do not hesitate to write out important quotations that you do not want to risk forgetting. In fact, even with an outline, it is advisable to write out your conclusion in full, because of the enduring impact that this final part has on the sermon and the gathered listeners. It is well known that a preacher's mind tires by the time they reach the end, and therefore, they risk an inarticulate ending to the sermon rather than a clear and articulate conclusion.

The third method is to preach without a manuscript or notes, relying almost exclusively on memory. The advantage of this method is that the preacher is completely free to connect with and engage the audience without any barriers or distractions. The disadvantage is that the unpracticed preacher will find that this degree of freedom can easily lead to tangents and ramblings that were never intended. It goes without saying that such a sermon can only be delivered by a highly skilled preacher with a honed memory. It calls for a disciplined preacher who can stick to the text without the text, so to speak. If you choose this method, then keep the following points in mind. After you have memorized your sermon, practice it at least three times without any text to gain the confidence to preach this way. When memorizing your sermon, construct a developing image, such as a table with four legs, which appears in your mind. For every major phase of the sermon, imagine that table coming together piece by piece so that you can keep track of where you are and how much farther you need to go. By associating the parts of your sermon with your visualization, you can better navigate your way through the time of the sermon. Lastly, you may want to keep a small sheet on hand, nonetheless, where major quotations can be written down in advance. Better to be safe than sorry.

None of these forms of preaching is exclusively good or bad. Their worth really depends on the experience and comfort of the preacher. You will find great preachers who preach using all three methods. Moreover, a preacher might find that a different method is more appropriate for different weeks. For example, if you are preaching on a topic in which you have expertise, then perhaps the third method will work best. However, if you are preaching on a new topic with material you are using for the first time, then the first method might be best for that week.

In terms of practicing the delivery of your sermon, it is helpful to mock-preach at least three times. The first time, preach your sermon in front of a mirror. As self-conscious as you might feel, it gives you a solid idea of whether the content of your sermon is matching up properly with your preaching style. For the second time, preach in front of a reliable and honest friend who can offer critical feedback about content, style, and voice. They will see and hear things you do not. One's spouse can potentially play this role very effectively. For the third time, preach as you intend to preach, this time imagining an audience in front of you. As you deliver the sermon, be attentive to the register and volume of your voice, the gestures and movement of your body, and your posture and orientation. This will help you focus on developing the right voice for the right sermon, which is an essential aspect of preaching, as we shall discuss in the following section.

Preaching with Style

The successful preacher will be able to do two things when they stand before an audience: (1) command near absolute attention focused on the message of the sermon and (2) be able to direct the mood of the audience to achieve the sermon's intended effect. To accomplish these two goals, attention must be given to three aspects of delivery: the physical setting, voice and speech patterns, and body language.

Physical Setting

When it comes to the physical setting, oftentimes the preacher's hands are tied unless they also manage or contribute to the management of the site in question. As a result, this section is most pertinent to the administrators of places of worship. There are four aspects of physical setting that contribute positively to the attention and mood of the audience:

1. *Seating Arrangement.* The first aspect concerns the seating arrangement of the congregation. The best possible arrangement for group cohesion is a setting in which people are seated close together with the preacher in close proximity. A large room with a thin, scattered group of attendees is a preacher's worst nightmare. However, in such a situation, the preacher can politely and skillfully request that the congregation come closer together.
2. *The Stage of Delivery.* The second aspect concerns the appearance of the pulpit, stage, podium, or whatever else might be the case. This aspect of the physical setting can significantly affect the mood. If the purpose is to create a sense of awe for the preacher, then a raised and decorated *minbar,* or platform, is appropriate. But if the intention is to create a sense of closeness, connectedness, and accessibility to the preacher, then a minimalist setup is more appropriate. Other moods can be created through the setting. Beautiful calligraphy can induce contemplation. Austere but well-kept white walls can accentuate a feeling of serenity. Places of worship usually have a standard appearance such that a few careful design choices can facilitate the desired mood. When possible, avoid pulpits and other structures that obstruct the congregation's view of the preacher. When flexibility is afforded, that is an opportunity to be creative. One can truly transform the setting in a manner appropriate to the event.
3. *Lighting.* Properly illuminating a site of worship can significantly change the feel of a place. In general, good lighting will help maintain alertness on the part of the congregation and possibly even foster a

mood of illumination. Harsh, bright lights or excessive sunlight, especially when shining in the eyes of those gathered, can be more of a distraction than a benefit for both preacher and audience. Insufficient lighting, in contrast, can dull the senses and put those in attendance to sleep. As a result, darkness and dimness should be avoided. While this is ideally the responsibility of the administrator or manager of the site, the preacher should be cognizant of how lighting affects an audience and should be ready to request more or less lighting as needed and if possible.

4. *Temperature.* A site that is too hot or too cold serves neither the preacher nor the congregation. An appropriate temperature is important in maintaining an audience's concentration; otherwise, agitation can quickly set in. In many cases, site managers set room temperatures in response to the temperature outdoors, unmindful of the actual climate inside. All too often, if it is extremely cold outside, the heat is turned up excessively. Yet the attendees will find the space uncomfortably hot, since they will have come in from the cold dressed in multiple layers. The opposite scenario can be true when sweltering hot weather outdoors prompts an overcompensation in the running of the air-conditioning.

Of course, many times these aspects of the physical settings cannot be changed, and the preacher will find themselves preaching in a less than ideal environment. As such, it would benefit the preacher to be sufficiently in tune with the congregation to know when physical settings are too great of an obstacle to overcome. In this situation, the preacher should be prepared to shorten their address out of a spirit of compassion and a desire to maintain attention. It is reported that the Prophet ﷺ would shorten his prayers and addresses when he heard the cry of an infant. There is much wisdom in this report for the preacher.

Voice and Patterns of Speech

Voice and speech patterns are distinct features of excellent preaching. A preacher's voice and general style of speaking greatly determine how much attention the audience will pay to the message. There are five aspects of voice and speech patterns that a preacher can employ to emphasize a point or capture an audience's attention:

1. *Repetition.* Repetition is a powerful way of driving home a point. A skilled preacher will not just simply repeat something thrice but will do it with varying tones, postures, and eye contact. When repetition is joined with style, something unforgettable is created. It is well known that the Prophet Muhammad ﷺ would often repeat words or sentences three times when he wanted to emphasize a particular teaching. The benefit of repetition is that it has the potential to create a lasting echo in the minds and hearts of listeners so that what has been said is with them long after the sermon has been delivered. The Qur'an makes use of repetition as well. For example, in *sūrat al-Raḥmān*, Allah asks over and over, *Which, then, of the blessings of your Lord will you deny?* (Q. 55:13).[5] Repetition can also mean repeating the same idea or teaching in different ways. Making ten different points in a sermon is less effective than making one point in ten different ways.
2. *Silence.* The wise preacher knows how and when to use silence effectively. The benefit of silence is twofold. First, it gives time for a deep question or profound statement to sink in as the audience reflects. Second, when set in contrast to the spoken word, silence can refocus attention between transitions. There is, however, a difference between effective silence and ineffective silence. An effective silence is when a preacher pauses intentionally but remains engaged physically, conscious of their countenance, gaze, and posture. Ineffective silence is when a preacher falls silent unintentionally or disengages to look over notes or the like. Keep in mind that the preacher always imagines the period of silence to be much longer and more awkward than it really is. Give silence an opportunity to work its charm. Do not be too eager to interrupt the congregation's moment of reflection.
3. *Raising One's Voice.* The intelligent preacher will reserve this method of dramatically raising the voice for special occasions when the audience needs to be awakened to the fierce urgency of the present. It is only useful to use a raised voice for a very brief time. Gestures such as pounding upon the pulpit can aid in the dramatic effect that is created. Be sure, however, to lower your voice down after the point has been made. Once you raise your voice, it might be physically difficult to go back down, so take a breather to transition back to your regular speaking voice. All too often in settings for Muslim preaching,

preachers bark with a raised voice from beginning to end. As a result, it remains unclear what the preacher really wanted to emphasize. Furthermore, a raised voice might initially arouse alertness, but if sustained too long, it turns into an annoyance such that all benefit is lost.

4. *Variations in Speed and Pitch.* Variation is essential for maintaining an audience's attention. Be sure to constantly switch gears, sometimes speaking in a soft, gentle, or even hushed tone and at other times speaking with intense passion. Saying something slowly allows time to digest and reflect, while picking up the pace helps you transport the audience with a vivid and exciting illustration. Monotony is the preacher's worst enemy. Garrison offers this insight: "A listener can go to sleep almost as easily when the preacher shouts in a monotone as when he murmurs monotonously."[6]
5. *Accessible Language.* Use shorter sentences and familiar words to keep an audience's attention without sacrificing deeper meanings. This is closely tied to writing a great sermon. Preaching experts advise the use of as many one- or two-syllable words as possible. As Garrison writes, "Any first-year theological student can be obscure; it takes ability and effort to present complex thoughts in simple sentences."[7]

Body Language

Effective preaching also requires the use of the entire body. The body language of a preacher is used to emphasize and visually illustrate the content of the sermon. Its appropriate use is key to maintaining the audience's attention. Garrison writes, "When the preacher is the only moving object in range of the listener's vision, his very movements will attract and re-attract flitting attention."[8] Body language is made up of three main components.

1. *Eye Contact.* The preacher connects with the audience using their eyes. And eye contact expresses more than words given the depth that our eyes can convey. When we squint and furrow our brow, we convey thought. When we close our eyes, we convey meditation and reflection. When we open our eyes wide, we convey enthusiasm, excitement, or emphasis. The eyes also maintain a preacher's connection with the audience. Therefore, never allow your eyes to wander aimlessly, looking up above or beyond where the audience is.

2. *Gestures of the Body and Hands.* Gestures are extensions of the emotions that the preacher brings and that the preacher desires the congregation to feel. Be conscious, then, of your movement and habitual ticks. The type of gestures that a preacher employs should depend on the situation. The employment of a variety of gestures throughout a sermon is more engaging than a limited few. Thus, if a preacher is trying to make a passionate plea for social justice, for instance, then the hand and body movement should be working in tandem to convey this point. On the other hand, if a preacher wants to convey a sober reality, then another style entirely is more appropriate. Many preachers make the mistake of employing just one type of gesture from beginning to end regardless of content or context, such as exaggerated hand movements. Such gesticulations lose their efficacy quickly and can even be distracting for the audience. Just as a monotone register is the worst voice to employ in preaching, a spare gestural repertoire is the worst type of body language that a preacher can bring to bear.
3. *Gestural Illustrations.* Using one's hands to evoke imagery can be both memorable and effective in preaching. The goal here is not so much to stir emotion but rather to evoke the human imagination. In prophetic preaching, we find the Prophet Muhammad ﷺ using this method often in his teachings. For example, in a well-attested hadith, "the Messenger of God ﷺ said, 'I and those who care for orphans will be in the Garden like this,' indicating with the slight gap between his forefinger and middle finger."[9] Similarly, in another report, "the Prophet ﷺ said, 'A believer to another believer is like a building whose parts reinforce each other.' The Prophet then clasped his hands with the fingers interlaced."[10] So preachers, likewise, can visually demonstrate their points with their hands to convert words of wisdom into unforgettable imagery. For instance, if a preacher were to say something like "We need to approach our religion in a way that intertwines spirituality and law," they could then clasp their hands dramatically together to make a more lasting impression.

A note of caution, however, is offered for this entire section on preaching with style. All the elements of preaching style—physical setting, voice and speech pattern, and body language—need to be practiced, honed, and developed over time. Every preacher will have a style and range of ability that comes naturally to them, but the task of a good preacher is to move beyond what is comfortable to incorporate new ways of effectively communicating. These new skills might feel awkward and unnatural at first, but when they are practiced enough, they can become second nature. At the same time, do not rush the process. Use your new skills in formal preaching slowly and wisely so that you do not come off as uncomfortable or unseasoned. Sometimes the content of a sermon can be great, but if it is not conveyed naturally and comfortably, its efficacy might fall short in the eyes of the congregation. Finally, it is worth reiterating that the key lesson of this section is that a diverse, contrasting array of styles is what makes the preaching experience vibrant and wholesome. As Garrison writes, "Indeed, it is safe to say that the most important single element in commanding attention is contrast or ordered change."[11]

Overcoming Obstacles to Good Preaching

No matter how much a preacher prepares for their address, uncontrollable factors exist that may affect the effectiveness of a sermon. As Garrison writes, "For the preacher it is significant that every such stimulus is a competitor."[12] Anticipating some of those factors can help the preacher maintain their calm and connection with the audience despite unwanted interferences. Here are some of the more common uncontrollable distractions for which you should prepare.

Noise

Noise can intrude in various ways and with different levels of intensity. For example, a crying baby or unruly children are particularly common, as are cell phones and sirens. Instinctually, a preacher may want to drown out the noise by speaking louder. In reality, this does nothing but add to the woe, as the noise for the audience just intensifies overall. Other ways may be used to deal with noise effectively. A preacher may try to incorporate the noise into the sermon in either a serious or humorous way. This, obviously, requires skill, but if a preacher is able to manage it, the benefit is that the audience refocuses on the sermon now that the noise and preaching have become one. There are reports that the Beloved of Allah ﷺ would embrace and pick up his grandchildren, Ḥasan and al-Ḥusayn, may Allah be well pleased with them, while he was in the midst of preaching. This seems to indicate an incorporating method for distractions. Alternatively, the preacher might lower their voice or become completely silent until the noise fades away. By creating contrast, the audience's attention is regained.[13] Furthermore, if it is a noise that can be managed, then those responsible or able to quiet the noise will be jolted into action with this sudden contrast. A deliberate hush or silence might feel awkward, but that time will be quickly forgotten once the noise dissipates and the sermon resumes. Of course, these are not foolproof solutions, but they can be helpful to keep in mind.

Latecomers

The problem of late arrivals is something that is almost always a distraction for the American *khaṭīb*, given that members of congregations are constantly pouring in as they travel from work, home, and school. As is often the case, the audience is quite thin at the beginning of the Friday address, while the place of worship is jam-packed by the end of it. There are two problems to consider here. First, latecomers can be distracting as they walk between lines or start praying their *sunna* prayers in front of people who were sitting and listening attentively. Second, those who come late to the *khuṭba* miss a good portion of the content of the sermon and may leave with misunderstandings having received only part of the message. As for the first matter, this is a physical setting issue that can be resolved with cooperation from a good administration. The congregation should be required to sit and fill the frontmost rows first so that when people come in late, they can join or form new rows behind them without being a distraction. Furthermore, this way those who come late will not end up praying their *sunna* prayers in front of those who are listening. This situation implies the need for educating the community on the proper etiquette of mosque entry as well. The arrival of latecomers also makes the conclusion of the sermon even more important in the American context. It is an opportunity not only to drive home the point but to repeat the main point or central teaching of the sermon so that latecomers can also benefit from the address.

Divided Spaces

Another obstacle the *khaṭīb* faces in many places of worship is that women in the congregation are often separated from the main hall by either a curtain or a barrier or are sectioned off in an entirely different space. This is challenging for the preacher because not everyone in the congregation will be able to share in the embodied preaching experience, where subtle nonverbal cues and body language may be lost. It is also, of course, a challenge for women as well, since they might not be able to see the expressions, movements, and gestures of the preacher or have a meaningful visual connection with the rest of the congregation. This can leave women feeling disconnected from the sermon and the Friday prayer experience altogether.

The administration of the site of worship ought to take the needs of women into proper consideration. When possible, administrators should seriously consider designing a main prayer hall large enough so that women can comfortably worship in the same space and be part of the preaching experience as fully as possible. Alternatively, an overlooking balcony area can also give women privacy while allowing them to be part of the preaching experience in a different way. If this is not possible due to space limitations or religious sensibilities, then at the very least excellent audio and visual technology should be used so that women can benefit from the *khuṭba* to some degree. In such a situation, the *khaṭīb*, even if new to a place, bears some responsibility as well. When a *khaṭīb* is faced with a physical setting that separates women entirely, then the *khaṭīb* needs to work with the administrators to ensure that the audio and video systems are working well. This reminds the administrators of their duty to the entire congregation or at least prompts them to think and move in the right direction. Essentially, a good *khaṭīb* must play the role of an advocate who seeks to make the worship service inclusive for everyone. Also, recalling the previous chapter, the *khaṭīb* ought to employ gender-inclusive language without fail and employ illustrations that connect with women as much as those that connect with men. As a note of caution, many well-known stories of the past are male-centric in their telling and orientation, so reflect well on how to use them if at all.

Time Management

Since Muslims do not typically have the day off on Friday in North America, time management of the *khuṭba* can be particularly challenging. A *khuṭba* that goes over the scheduled time runs the risk of not only losing people's attention but also quite possibly upsetting and even angering those who need to return to work or class. An inconsiderate *khaṭīb* might argue that religious instruction is more important than worldly matters, but many congregants have inflexible jobs that they cannot afford to lose or compromise. The pressure to keep on time is a good pressure to have, as it forces the wise *khaṭīb* to preach efficiently. However, there are times when the factor of time becomes an even greater obstacle, such as arriving at the place of worship late due to traffic, poor management at the site of worship that causes a delayed beginning, or bad weather that requires the service to end sooner than expected. As such, when you are writing and preparing your sermon, it is always good to make a physical or mental note of paragraphs or points that you could do without while keeping your core message intact just in case the need arises to shorten your address unexpectedly. If you have prepared a point-by-point type *khuṭba*, you should consider how you might reduce the number of points to something less.

Unfamiliarity

Another challenge that the typical American *khaṭīb* faces is a lack of familiarity with the congregation to whom they are tasked to preach, since most places of worship have rotating preachers rather than a regular one. Preachers will often find themselves preaching in a place where they only know a single administrator or board member. There are two problems that arise out of this situation. First, the *khaṭīb* may say something offensive or irrelevant due to this lack of familiarity. Second, the audience may not entirely trust this new or unfamiliar *khaṭīb.* As for the first problem, it is the preacher's responsibility to find out as much as possible about the congregation before the time of the sermon. You should ask pointedly if there are any sensitivities or sensibilities that you should be aware of and if there are any pertinent issues facing the community that you should keep in mind as you choose your topic. As for the second problem, the best way to establish credibility and trust with the audience is with a strong opening. The Arabic invocations that begin the *khuṭba* should be as close to perfect as possible. Stumbling through any part of the *khuṭba* can completely turn off many listeners. Also, offering a personal story early in the sermon can help establish a relationship where there was none before or at least elicit a sense of familiarity.

Reading the Congregation

Lastly, in many Muslim settings, it is difficult for the preacher to gauge whether or not the congregation is connecting with the message, since the audience is sitting on the floor often looking downward with blank expressions. To make matters worse, no matter how good a sermon is, the preacher can almost always find someone who has fallen asleep or someone who is completely distracted. Preachers are generally at their best when they can feed off the congregation's energy. Thus, when the preacher is faced with an obstacle like this, it is easy to become doubtful or lose motivation altogether. Anytime the preacher wants the sermon to be over, you know the audience is thinking the same thing. The first thing to do is to focus your gaze on the few people who do respond to the sermon with full attention, nods, smiles, and the rest. Try to identify at least one person in each field of view—left, right, and straight ahead—so that you can make eye contact with every part of the congregation. Focusing your attention on the attentive will give you the motivation to preach on, as it were. There is a natural tendency, out of nervousness and self-doubt, to focus on the inattentive when preaching, but that is a disservice to yourself and to those who enthusiastically receive your message.

Ethics of the Pulpit

A preacher's efforts to preach a great sermon must always be tempered with good ethics. On this front, we offer five ethical points to which every preacher upon the pulpit ought to commit.

Never Lie from the Pulpit

The congregation places enormous trust in the preacher. Therefore, a preacher must exhibit utmost honesty from the pulpit. It is from this concern for truthfulness that a preacher never plagiarizes a sermon. In general, be wary of reading other people's sermons instead of writing and developing your own. A generic *khuṭba* taken from some book never does justice to the local concerns and contexts of a people. For this reason, this guide—unlike many other preaching guides—avoids "sample" sermons. The whole point of this handbook is to help preachers prepare and deliver sermons in their own voices.

Shun Sensationalism

Shun the practice of sensationalizing from the pulpit. Perform your preaching duties with a sense of integrity, decency, and dignity. Never feign weeping or anger or even humbleness. Be straight with the people, and they will respect you and your message. If you truly become emotional, then let it be, but never dramatize emotion to gain your intended effect. According to Berkey, dramatic confessions such as seeing the Prophet in a dream were quite common happenings among preachers in Muslim history, but over time it undermined the credibility of the entire vocation rather than strengthening it.[14] Hoyt argues that the problem with sensationalism is that "it puts the man before the message" and this type of preaching may "trumpet the preacher's name by the lips of thousands, but that might not work for righteousness and establish the kingdom of spiritual life."[15] It is precisely this—the cult of personality over message—that needs to be avoided today as well.

Maintain Trust

Never divulge the secrets of another person from the pulpit. A preacher is often sought as a counselor or confidant. People will tell the preacher things that they may not even share with their own family and friends. Hold this trust in high esteem. Never let there even be a sliver of doubt that you are exposing someone's secrets. I have heard many preachers begin stories like "The other day, a man came to me and asked me . . ." Now, the preacher may think that this is harmless because a name was not mentioned in the story, but people will never confide in you if they fear that their secrets will form the contents of your sermons!

Respect the Dignity of the Pulpit

Never abuse or misuse your position on the pulpit. The purpose of the sermon is to remind and teach the community, not to promote one's own agenda or self-interests. Never discuss your disagreements with *masjid* administrators or the like in the sermon or talk about things that are of a personal nature. Also, a preacher should only accept financial compensation as is appropriate for a dignified livelihood and should seek other means of wealth, if possible, since the mixing of preaching and wealth can result in corruption.[16]

Call Not to Extremes

Never use the pulpit to preach extremism. It is completely unacceptable for a preacher to preach hate toward any group of people—Muslim or non-Muslim—or to call people to stand for justice other than by nonviolent means. A preacher must never ask people to do things that are extreme and that they would later come to regret, such as leaving behind a spouse and children to go on a missionary-style trip or leaving school or a career to devote oneself purely to religious knowledge. A preacher must always consider and weigh well the consequences of their words and teachings upon individual listeners, their families, and the larger society.

The Evaluation Process: Learn and Grow

To become a great preacher, a preacher must learn how to seek and accept critical feedback. Preaching is truly an art, and like every other form of art, it requires immense time, effort, and criticism to achieve beauty. In the sciences, there is a saying: "Practice makes perfect." The same cannot be said of the arts, since there is always room for growth, and there is no such thing as perfection. Likewise, preaching is an art and not a science. Three forms of evaluation can benefit the preacher.

Self-Evaluation

The preacher ought to take some time after they preach to consider carefully how the preaching experience went. What aspects turned out well, and what aspects could have been improved? Usually, a preacher can feel in their gut whether the sermon was well delivered. But the real question the preacher needs to ask themselves is whether the sermon has had any effect on their own behavior or understanding. If so, then thank Allah for a job well done. If not, then work needs to be done to improve your sermon. When the preacher is inspired and changed by their own preaching, this is the greatest success.

Audience Evaluation

If a preacher remains long enough after their sermon, they will always receive some sort of feedback, be it good or bad. Intention matters greatly here. The preacher must be careful not to do so in search of praise alone. People are usually too kind and courteous to criticize your sermon to your face, so even when someone praises your sermon, ask for criticism, and push them to offer you something in the form of constructive criticism. Seeking genuine feedback is a good habit. Close friends and family members can especially serve as honest evaluators. Make it clear to your close associates that you want to hear both the good and the bad and that their evaluation is a service to the community. Be sure to seek evaluations from different segments of your community—across ethnic, gender, and generational lines—so that you can get a fuller sense of the effectiveness of your preaching.

Community-Wide Systematic Evaluation

This form of evaluation is best organized by other members of the community rather than preachers. Community leaders should develop some sort of mechanism whereby the congregation can anonymously offer feedback every week.

Anonymity here is key. Given the general accessibility of smart devices and computers, gathering such feedback is even easier. Upon completion, these evaluations should be shared with the *khaṭīb* on a regular basis. Every institution can develop its own questions depending on its circumstances, but it is essential to receive feedback on the clarity and effectiveness of content, delivery, and the overall preaching experience.

Nevertheless, to be completely honest, receiving feedback—especially criticism—is never easy. It can be quite hurtful to one's ego and can lead to a weakening of morale. Without critical feedback, however, the preacher can never grow in their vocation. Therefore, a spirit of humbleness is always needed when pursuing all three forms of evaluation. What is also needed, at the same time, is the wisdom to discern which feedback is useful and how the feedback you receive will affect your future preaching, if at all. Not every piece of advice you receive will be good advice, so take the time to discern your core principles and values so that you can properly judge and assess the evaluation.

5 On Women and the Friday Prayer Service

MUCH HAS BEEN SAID ABOUT THE preacher. In the preceding chapters, the focus, by and large, has been on the work and character of the *khaṭīb*, advice for preparing and delivering sermons, and strategies for managing some of the intrinsic and extrinsic factors of the preaching environment. Nevertheless, there are times when the forum of the sermon is insufficient for hearing and holding the community. Invariably, moments arise when a preacher must engage more directly with the community as greater issues and personal concerns come to reside in the hearts of its members. What those issues might be are manifold, as are the ways that we might address them.

This chapter aims to name and hold one set of concerns for careful consideration: the presence (or absence) of women in the Friday prayer service itself. How can the space of the Friday prayer service be made more inclusive for the women within our communities of faith? My time with the Princeton Muslim Life Program has offered me the opportunity to work through some of these concerns. While each community is different, the set of concerns named here is increasingly relevant for those of us preaching in an American Muslim context. I hope to share the experience of our community process as well as offer possible models aimed at enhancing the spiritual enrichment and contribution of both the women and men of a congregation.

Hearing and Holding the Community in Faith

> My whole philosophy around pastoral care is to be there to listen, to be there as a source of compassion, to be there as a source of helping

people listen to their inner voices and seek clarity from within by asking the right questions and by offering reflective counseling.
—*Sohaib Sultan, telephone interview by Harvey Stark, June 16, 2014*

Several years ago, I was approached with concerns over the role of women in the Friday prayer service. A group of young university students came to me as their chaplain to start a conversation on how we might rethink our Friday prayer service at Princeton University to be more gender inclusive. Their genuine concerns raised an important question: How could *jumuʿa,* the weekly celebration of our coming together in faith, be made more welcoming, encompassing, and spiritually empowering for the community's women and men?

The students who raised these questions were well intentioned and sincere. As they shared their perspectives and stories, those students revealed that there was a real hurt associated with not seeing women preach or partake in offering religious wisdom on this important occasion of the Friday prayer. "It's almost like we do not exist" was just one of the sentiments shared by these students. They did not feel represented. They did not feel like they truly belonged.

This feeling was not difficult to understand. Many of the visible roles performed during a typical Friday prayer service in North America (and beyond) are carried out by men. A male *muezzin* (or *muʾadhdhin*) will step forward to deliver the call to prayer. Sometimes, that same male voice is broadcast throughout the prayer space. A male reciter might fill the prayer soundscape with his recitation of the Qur'an. Then a male *khaṭīb* will stand before the entire congregation, deliver a sermon, and then lead the gathered attendees in congregational prayer. Oftentimes, in conclusion, a male figure will typically stand to relay a series of community announcements. As a result, the entire observance of the *jumuʿa* service reads male. Even the prayer space itself might be strongly gender-coded, depending on its spatial configuration. In many prayer spaces, women pray behind men, are partitioned off, or sometimes sit completely out of sight in separate rooms or even buildings, as I noted in the preceding chapter. It is unsurprising, then, that the women of a congregation would have a difficult time seeing themselves within the ritual celebration of the Friday prayer service. If their very person is not being represented, can they expect their views and concerns to be adequately represented as well? As Ingrid Mattson poignantly and incisively writes,

When few or no women in a community have recognized spiritual authority or positions of leadership, however, there is a good chance that the women of that community will experience religious authority negatively. This is a serious matter, because it defeats the very purpose of religious institutions, whose primary purpose is to bring people closer to God. We need to be conscious of the unfortunate reality that institutions—including religious institutions—often develop in ways that lead them to defeat the very purposes they were created to serve.[1]

No institution is immune to this danger. How could the Muslim Life Program, then, engage this issue in a productive and faithful way? If the voiced concerns were to be taken seriously, we had to turn to spaces beyond the *khuṭba*.

First, it was important for the voices of these students to feel and be heard. We embarked together on a series of open discussions to work collectively toward a reasonable balance. Our initial conversations were respectful and honest, which set an important tone early on. Then I convened town hall meetings where the larger community could join in to discuss everyone's concerns and consider possible alternatives. We were looking for models of practice that we might implement that were respectful of the broad goal of inclusivity while still being permissible within the disclosed parameters of the *Shari'ah*, or Sacred Law. It was a long process, as it should be, of discernment and collective thinking. Together we debated and discussed the matter in consultation with Islamic scholars from a wide range of schools of thought in search of creative solutions. After all, this was more than a matter of symbolic positioning or performative window-dressing. This was a matter of the spiritual well-being of our community of faith.

How Muslims have engaged and continue to engage with their faith varies widely across time and place. The modes of devotion observed and paths for spiritual enrichment pursued are manifold. The manner of our religious formation often attunes us to particular repertoires of worship and spiritual practice. Prayer, of course, runs through all these many repertoires as a common thread binding them together. After all, prayer is a central pillar for the life of faith. As the Prophet Muhammad ﷺ relates, "Islam is built upon five [pillars]: Witnessing that there is no god but God and that Muhammad is the Messenger of God, the establishment of the prayer, the giving of the prescribed charity, pilgrimage to the House, and fasting in Ramadan."[2] Indeed, prayer has an existential quality across creation. As God proclaims in the Qur'an, *Whosoever is in the heavens and earth prostrates to God, willingly or unwillingly, as do their shadows in the morning and evening* (Q. 13:15). Even to the eyes of outsiders, the ritual prayer is iconic and defining.

Prayer, of course, takes many forms and shapes. Subtle variations inflect our prayers—variations informed by upbringing, our traditions of religious formation, and careful juristic discernment. We can also pray alone, alongside our families, or with a congregation, even if only a small number are present. To this last end, mosques represent those sites of congregation where others can be found to pray alongside. Following the precedent set by the Prophet Muhammad ﷺ, we strive to congregate in our houses of worship to pray in unison.

Nevertheless, the importance that the mosque has for women varies widely across the Muslim world. In some settings and situations, women rarely go to the mosque at all. Cultural norms and access often play a significant role. In other cases, that lack of affinity might be based on the interpretation of certain prophetic traditions, or hadiths, that elevate the home as a site of worship for women instead. For instance, in *Sunan Abī Dāwūd*, the Prophet ﷺ reportedly states, "It is more excellent for a woman to pray in her house than in her courtyard, and more excellent for her to pray in her private chamber than in her house."[3] In other settings and situations, the case is the opposite. In these cultural contexts, women attend the mosque regularly with different cultural norms and traditions shaping preference and predilection. There are numerous prophetic reports, or hadiths, that relate that the Prophet Muhammad ﷺ said, "Do not prevent the female servants of Allah from going to the mosque."[4] Indeed, the array of historical precedents, Qur'anic injunctions, and this subset of hadiths may well be read to encourage regular worship at the mosque, especially the *jumu'a* service. Even setting aside considerations of religious obligations, many women seek out mosques anyway for the spiritual upliftment and religious edification that the communities there can provide. There is power in believing *with* a community. Whatever the case may be elsewhere in the world, in the American Muslim context, where Muslims are a distinct religious minority, many women see the mosque and its Friday prayer service as an important space and time for spiritual formation and community building. As a result, many women and men expect mosques in North America to be more welcoming and inclusive to all within their communities. Can the spiritual voice of women, then, be included and celebrated in the *jumu'a* space and experience—a space and experience that have been largely male-dominated for centuries? From my personal observation, this probing question exists especially in communities where young people are present and actively looking for greater gender equity.

Exploring the Precedents of the Past

The concerns surrounding women and the Friday prayer service are hardly new. They have persisted for generations, especially within American Muslim settings. However, when a woman-led Friday prayer service of a mixed-gender congregation was held in New York City in 2005, the raft of issues alluded to above gained greater prominence in the American Muslim imagination, especially given the attention that the event received from major media outlets and social media networks.[5] Religious scholars and community faith leaders across North America and beyond weighed in about the service's permissibility, its meaning, its implications, and what it revealed about women, religious practice, and authority at a broader level. With so many significant discussions taking place and seeding the religious environment, it was unsurprising that the students at Princeton raised their concerns to me. Part of the process for engaging with our questions around women and the Friday prayer service was to study the precedents of the Islamic past.

Historically, there is a long and rich tradition of women religious authorities who taught and preached in public in front of both men and women. Reports have been preserved by Muslim scholars in a wide array of sources from biographical dictionaries and historical chronicles to classical works of hadith, Qur'anic exegesis, spirituality, and law, among many other sources. Meticulous research has fed a growing body of scholarship aimed at revealing the shape and extent of women's involvement in the religious sciences, as both students and scholars. Women led assemblies of learning, taught texts, and transmitted hadiths. For example, Asma Sayeed has brought to light many of the learned women involved in the study and transmission of hadiths across the first eight centuries of Islam, especially during the scholarly resurgence of women from the fourth ḥijrī century onward.[6] Similarly, Aisha Geissinger has analyzed the various female authorities cited by early scholars of Qur'anic interpretation and compilers of hadith.[7] In an extensive, wide-ranging historical study, Marion Katz gathers and presents one of the more impressive collections of historical attestations from across many centuries and regional contexts, concerning the presence and activity of women within the mosque, especially with respect to religious learning and teaching.[8]

To offer some illustrative examples, Sayeed describes the life of Karīma al-Marwaziyya (d. ca. 463/1070), a famed female hadith transmitter of Khurāsān and Mecca who studied with prominent scholars and "attracted numerous students to her assemblies," where she related to them her extensive knowledge of hadith.[9] In fact, she was a noted transmitter of al-Bukhārī's important collection of *ṣaḥīḥ* prophetic reports.[10] Several centuries later in Mamluk Damascus, Zaynab bint al-Kamāl (d. 740/1339) presided over dozens of gatherings for the reading of hadith collections and the transmission of other religious works. Among her students were prominent scholars such as al-Dhahabī (d. 748/1348), al-Subkī (d. 771/1369–70), and Ibn Baṭṭūṭa (d. 770/1368–69 or 779/1377).[11] Jonathan Brown relates how the famed Ibn Taymiyya (d. 728/1328) regarded with respect the Hanbalī scholar Fātima bint ʿAbbās (d. 714/1315), who "took to the pulpits of Damascus mosques to harangue and inspire a sinful public with her preaching."[12] These examples of women scholars publicly engaged in the transmission of religious knowledge were more common than is typically recognized by our communities today. Emphasizing how prevalent female legal scholars were in later centuries, Mirjam Künkler writes,

> Women jurists can be found from Timbuktu to Cairo, from Damascus to Baghdad, and from Isfahan and Nishapur, from the 700s to the 1500s and across the Hanafi, Hanbali, Maliki, Shafi'i, and Shia schools of law. Nor is there evidence that women transmitted or taught only on gender-specific themes. The Shafi'i jurist Amīnā bint al-Ḥusayn al-Maḥāmilī (d. 987) was particularly expert in the law of inheritance. The Hanbali jurist Fatimah bint 'Abbas ibn Abi al-Fath al-Baghdadiyyah al-Hanbaliyyah (d. 1333) became a renowned scholar of the Quran, and her contemporary, the great Islamic scholar Ibn Taymiyah, acknowledged her as an equal in knowledge and expertise. 'A'isha bint 'Abd al-Hadi al-Ba'uniya (d. 1516) excelled in Arabic grammar and rhetoric, Islamic law, theology, and mysticism.[13]

Katz's wide-ranging historical study of women's mosque activities offers an even wider lens into how Muslim women have figured into the life of the mosque across Islamic history. As she summarizes, women "frequented mosques to participate in congregational prayer, to celebrate the great nocturnal festivals of the medieval Islamic calendar, to hear preaching, to teach, to socialize, and to rest."[14] While the frequency, degree of access, and even resistance to such activities varied widely from place to place, and even mosque to mosque, this rich array of attestations from the past points nevertheless to the many diverse ways that women have found enrichment and spiritual uplift in their houses of worship. Indeed, a number of important studies have drawn attention to the many ways that Muslim women have pursued their religiosity today. Saba Mahmoud has analyzed the Cairene women's mosque movement, Pieternella van Doorn-Harder has studied the educational networks of women religious leaders in Indonesia, Feryal Salem has documented the acclaimed women religious scholars of modern-day Damascus, and Maria Jaschok and Shui Jingjun Shui have traced the history of women-exclusive mosques in China.[15]

However, there are few examples, in the past or present, of women serving as the *khaṭīb* during a *jumu'a* service anywhere in the world. The reasons for this are manifold and explored elsewhere.[16] Nonetheless, a segment of the Muslim community in America is passionately arguing for the inclusion of women *khaṭībs*, usually as part of a larger concern for equality in women's access to and representation within the mosque. After all, women naturally bring another set of perspectives on texts and traditions that can help broaden the religious understanding of the congregation and expand their opportunities for illumination. Nevertheless, the opposition to this position is equally ardent in its desire to preserve the established worship life of the community. From a pastoral perspective, the cohesion and spiritual well-being of the community is key. How can major divisions or even fractious splits be avoided so that a thriving and happy community is fostered instead? How might the voice and presence of women be granted greater prominence in other ways?

During our rich conversations and consultations, we learned a great deal about what had come before with respect to women and worship. We also came to better appreciate what was religiously possible and what we, as a community, would be willing to explore. We were ready, then, to gradually try out and implement a number of different practices within the space of the Friday prayer service that might answer the questions raised above. What I describe below was not imposed from above but developed in collaboration with my community at Princeton. These were steps that had to be shepherded with care, formed with constant and open conversation, and carried out with open hearts.

Engaging the Tradition within the Muslim Life Community at Princeton

Here are brief summaries of a few models of practice we developed that were worth exploring within the context of our community.

The *Bayān* Model

Interestingly, it is the long, reliable, and accepted history of women preaching and teaching in public settings outside of the formal Friday prayer service that gave us an opening. In South Asia and other non-Arabic–speaking Muslim societies, many legal scholars consider the *khuṭba*, or sermon, to be a necessary component of the *jumuʿa* prayer service and one that must be delivered in Arabic. The reasoning is that only an Arabic-language *khuṭba* upholds the *Sunna*, or tradition of the Prophet Muhammad ﷺ. Just as the prayer itself is performed in Arabic, so must be the sermon, regardless of the local language spoken by the worshipping community. Of course, this presented a major dilemma because in many of these communities, most of the congregation could not understand the message of the sermon. As such, these same legal scholars introduced the delivery of a *bayān*, or spiritual address, immediately before the formal *jumuʿa* sermon. While the *bayān* would be in the local language for the sake of the non-Arabic–speaking congregation, the *khuṭba* itself would remain in Arabic.

This is how a typical Friday prayer service looks that includes a local language *bayān*. Generally, a wise (male) preacher offers the *bayān* at the start of the service. Because it is being delivered in the language of the people, the *bayān* is relatively longer. Many see it as the primary space where preachers can deliver their message. Once concluded, the call to prayer is given announcing the formal start of the *jumuʿa* service itself. At this point, a younger (male) preacher usually rises to offer the *khuṭba* in Arabic. This second sermon, intended simply to fulfill religious expectations, is generally kept short and sweet. After its brief delivery, the congregation rises to follow the preacher in the congregational Friday prayer.

A comparatively greater number of rulings and customs govern the formal Friday prayer service, such as the required language of the *khuṭba* (depending on one's school of thought) and arguably the gender of *khaṭīb* delivering it. Far fewer guidelines exist for the *bayān*. In fact, a few Islamic scholars advised us that we could try the following model of practice: both women and men could be invited to give a community-oriented *bayān*, while a male *khaṭīb* would deliver an abbreviated Arabic-language *khuṭba* and then lead the prayer. As the many historic examples above demonstrate, the *bayān*, or spiritual address, of women has been widely accepted in previous centuries across a range of Muslim social settings, whether these learned women were teaching law and hadith or preaching morals and matters of belief.

The *bayān* model is exciting and ripe with possibilities, even though its introduction required patience and care. That we were able to even raise the model as a possibility is likely due to the institutional setting itself, a college campus with a fairly secular, liberal orientation. A great deal of explaining, teaching, and answering questions was required. After undertaking this important groundwork, even the more skeptical and conservative members of our congregation continued to attend the Friday prayer service without fear over the service's validity. In the end, however, we turned to other options. Confusion over the model persisted to the point of causing enduring divisions within our community. Congregations are fluid. While many attended the town hall meetings, many others could only afford to stop by the Friday prayer itself. The learning and conversations that were needed could not be had by all. As much as we tried to educate and acclimatize, new reactions and encounters always arose. It was time for us to explore alternatives. After all, one of the main purposes of *jumuʿa*, the prayer service that literally brings us together, is to maintain the unity of our community.

The *Duʿāʾ* Model

Another creative practice that came out of our series of conversations is the practice of inviting a woman to offer a communal supplication, or *duʿāʾ*, after the conclusion of the ritual prayer each week. This idea originates from a spiritual tradition carried out by certain Sufi orders, or *ṭuruq*, in West Africa. These communities gather regularly to chant communally the remembrance of Allah, a practice known as *dhikr*. Typically, at the end of these sessions, women offer *duʿāʾ* to conclude the devotional gathering. Taking this practice as a model, we came up with the idea of having a woman give *duʿāʾ* at the end of our weekly Friday prayer service. This would offer women within the community the opportunity to contribute a spiritual and moral message through the supplications that they would compose and deliver. They could uplift different aspects of the faith or draw attention to considerations and concerns that the male *khaṭībs* might have neglected or been unable to address due to the constraints of time.

The women in our community who have undertaken this responsibility have offered beautiful, heartfelt *duʿā's*. Their supplications continually move us deeply. The practice has become a cherished part of the spiritual and worship life of our community. I can say, from my experience, that the women of our congregation have added very special voices, tones, perspectives, and attitudes that have been nothing but enriching. They have raised matters of the heart, mind, and society that are often missed or overlooked by their male counterparts. In fact, because of the fine balance that this practice has struck for us, it is the model that we have decided to adopt most wholeheartedly. In fact, in an appendix at the end of this book, I have reproduced several of the beautiful *duʿā's* that the women of our community have shared these past few years in hopes of inspiring others.

The Qur'anic Recitation and Translation Model

This last practice would complement well either of the above two models if implemented. Specifically, it draws on the celebrated tradition and art of women reciting the Qur'an publicly. Many Muslim women engage in public Qur'an recitation competitions across the Muslim world, especially in Southeast Asia. At Princeton, time is set aside at the beginning of each Friday prayer service for the recitation of the Qur'an. Ideally, we have tried to alternate between men and women for the weekly recitation. This practice allows for the voice of our women to beautify the *jumuʿa* experience and space. Moreover, the Qur'an need not be recited in Arabic alone. Another individual, female or male, can also be designated to read aloud the Qur'anic passage being recited in English afterward. Like the *bayān*, offering an English reading of the Qur'an helps give the community yet another point of engagement with faith and spiritual development.

• • •

In conclusion, our honest discussions and robust debates allowed us to explore several possibilities for women's voices to be positively included and celebrated in the *jumuʿa* experience and space. We found these practices to be in accord with the parameters of the Sacred Law while also easing the limitations that some in our community so deeply felt. I offer these models of practice in the spirit of pastoral care for the broader community of faith, fully recognizing that the larger religious debate surrounding the set of concerns initially raised falls beyond the scope of this book. May these suggestions be of benefit, *insha'Allah*.

My personal observations as the Muslim Chaplain at Princeton University have led me to conclude that there is something very beautiful and worthwhile in including and celebrating the voices of Muslim women at *jumuʿa*, whether it is in the form of Qur'an recitation at the beginning or the offering of a *duʿāʾ* at the end. The message of *jumuʿa* overall is meant to give the congregation perspective on both spiritual and social matters. Arguably, this cannot be done without the presence and voice of the women of our community, who constitute half of who we are. Think of all the women from among the generation of the Companions who addressed and engaged with our beloved Prophet Muhammad ﷺ in the early years of the faith. It is important, then, to bring women's voices to bear on the spiritual and social issues of our times today. We should be constantly asking ourselves how we can make our congregations as vibrant and dynamic as that early Muslim community of faith.

For our part in the Muslim Life Program at Princeton, we have found the models described above as having different measures of spiritual and social benefit. At the very least, they should represent possibilities for a community to consider and explore as it seeks more positive ways to include and elevate women without altogether altering what Muslims have come to expect and accept from the religious tradition. While the Muslim Life Program has developed and matured in response to this long, ongoing process, I also fully recognize that this is not the only way to respond to the initial set of concerns raised. Congregations and contexts vary immensely. What works at Princeton University will not necessarily work elsewhere. I also know that what might work best for my community presently will likely change with time. Each congregation will have to undertake its own process of discernment with great care and compassion. Just because the process will be difficult, however, does not mean that our community should ignore or avoid these very real concerns. Our spiritual well-being as a community is at stake. As I once said, "I think in our community we need to create more and more avenues in places where there is common agreement about the place and role of female preachers and teachers."[17]

And God knows best.

Conclusion

On Ways Forward

THE FRIDAY *KHUṬBA* SERVES AN ENORMOUSLY important role in the American Muslim community as a significant source of Islamic inspiration and knowledge on a weekly basis. It is critical, therefore, that we as a community seriously focus our attention on raising the state of our preaching in order to meet the needs of Muslims living in twenty-first-century America. Much of this preaching manual has focused on what individual preachers can do to improve their own preaching. Every *khaṭīb* has the responsibility to work on the effectiveness of their preaching, but the community as a whole has to provide the right resources to help preachers pursue their work better. This chapter seeks to open a conversation on how we can raise the standards of our Friday prayer services using community-based resources and institutions.

Developing the Right Resources for Great Preaching

Complaints about and criticisms of our Friday preaching are rampant, but little has been done to address or improve it. Part of the problem is that an apathetic attitude toward this issue prevails. We are content to complain but unready, so it seems, to take action. We have come to accept things as they are, not as they can be. If we hope for our communities to grow, then this state of affairs must change. I offer several suggestions here for what we can do at a community level to support great preaching. If we as a community can begin to pull our resources together for this purpose, it will send a strong message that preaching is important to us and also help set a vision of what we believe to be possible. Without a vision of what might be, what hope is there for taking Islamic preaching to the next level?

First of all, this book should not be seen as the last word on the matter of preaching. Instead, I hope that it is only among the first. We need many more books to join this one. What we need today is a growing library of literature on the life and art of preaching. One of the first projects that we need to undertake, then, is the development of a *series of books on Islamic preaching* that will examine the subject from various angles and contribute to the revival of preaching as a religious field of learning and as an art in the modern world. Three genres will be especially needed for this series of preaching guides.

To develop our future, we need to take stock of our past. To this end, we need studies aimed at surveying and studying the many preaching manuals that have been written throughout Islamic history. This is not only a matter of translating texts into English. We also need to translate that knowledge for our current cultural context in order to ensure its relevance. If properly pursued, Muslim preachers will be able to connect more intimately with the rich legacy of Islamic preaching while also gaining a greater appreciation for the place of preaching in Muslim discourses across generations. A proper historical understanding of our preaching tradition should inspire present-day preachers to take their vocation as seriously as any other field of study in Islamic thought.

Second, we need to conduct surveys, collect data, and compile statistics in order to clearly assess the current state of Islamic preaching in America. Hearsay and anecdotal evidence will not suffice. Instead, we need to interview a broad swath of American Muslim faith leaders to determine the challenges they face, the manner and process of their work, and the resources at their disposal. At the same time, it is important to interview congregations in order to determine what they are looking for from the pulpit. How are sermons being received? What services are needed? Where do they hope to go and grow? Collecting data will be important, but we must also analyze this data carefully with a mind toward formulating concrete recommendations. American Muslim faith leaders and their congregations need a better sense of the range of experiences and perspectives around them so that they can better support one another. Alongside this macrolevel research, more personalized studies are needed too. Our community is blessed with talented preachers. Close studies of prominent faith leaders would provide aspiring preachers and congregations with models to strive for as well.

Third, we need more guides that further develop the theory and art of Islamic preaching. We need guides that draw on the historical and statistical research that emerges out of the two previously discussed genres. In reality, every chapter of this preaching manual deserves further attention and consideration. More voices need to be shared along with different approaches to developing the art and life of preaching. While I have offered my advice here, I know we would benefit from many other perspectives. Seminary students and current preachers seeking self-improvement would benefit immensely from a series of well-written, easy-to-read, and succinct guides. Our community needs to expand the educational resources for preaching that are presently available.

Related to this is our need to develop a well-designed, user-friendly online portal for *khaṭībs* and other Muslim faith leaders. Christians have developed several resourceful networks, journals, and digital platforms dedicated to supporting and developing the art of preaching within their communities. Muslims can look to these models to develop our own authentic resources. What we need is a central site that serves as a directory, a repository, and a forum. We need a directory to connect preachers who live and work in remote parts of the country. We need a repository to collect and organize the many digital resources out there. The site can feature articles on how to approach difficult issues in preaching, compile effective illustrations for delivering a sermon, share tips and advice on preaching well in different institutional settings like schools or hospitals, and gather advice on how faith leaders can balance vocation and other life responsibilities, among many other possibilities. The benefit of such a portal, however, extends beyond practical matters. It would also provide a space for Muslim preachers to exchange ideas with one another across the country and encounter new ideas and thought-provoking perspectives. Such a digital platform would also go a long way to further the building and nurturing of a needed sense of community among Muslim faith leaders themselves. Maintaining such a portal will require some financial investment and dedicated staffing, but the outcomes will be well worth it for the community in the long term.

With respect to education, institutions like Hartford Theological Seminary (now Hartford International University) should develop courses on the art of Islamic preaching in order to train future Muslim faith leaders in America. These classes should carefully consider both the theory and practice of preaching. With respect to theory, the purpose of preaching and the many issues that emerge from it should be explored and expounded upon. With regard to practice, the focus should be on developing best practices for the writing and delivering of sermons. An ideal syllabus would allocate time to theoretical discussions while also allowing for mock preaching sessions that are critically evaluated by instructors and peers. Online classes on preaching would also be useful to reach preachers farther afield, especially those in more remote parts of the country. Naturally, such a course needs to tackle what Islamic preaching in twenty-first-century America requires and what good preaching looks like in our rapidly shifting institutional settings. This subject is especially important for preachers newly arrived in the United States who are struggling to familiarize themselves with their new context.

The design of an intensive preaching seminar that covers core concepts in the art of preaching is also needed. Such a seminar could be taught over a weekend and made to travel to a variety of locales. An abundance of sources, this book included, could be used to develop this workshop. The primary purpose would be to expose as many communities as possible to the tools that make for good preaching, effective faith leaders, and supportive congregants. The materials used in this weekend seminar should be accessible enough for any community to engage with while offering enough depth and discussion to be memorable and worthwhile for attendees. More than a series of lectures, such a seminar needs to be immersive and interactive.

All of the proposals that I have put forth in this section require serious commitment and financial investment from our leading institutions and communities. This is the only way to improve the state of preaching on a wide scale across communities. Preaching standards cannot be imposed by any one person or organization in America. Higher standards are generated by the expectations developed by local communities and within the circles of faith leaders themselves. When the right resources are directed toward developing the art of preaching, it is only a matter of time before great preaching becomes a more widespread reality. When this happens, the field will self-discriminate in a way that draws in hardworking preachers and sidelines those who do not develop themselves. I saw this happen with my own eyes in one community. When that community began to take seriously its standards for good preaching, it began investing in a *khaṭīb* training program and other supportive elements. As a result, there was a significant and palpable improvement in the community's Friday sermons. Once standards are raised and a congregation experiences great preaching, the community will not expect anything less and the community of preachers, in turn, will push one another week after week to raise the bar.

Think Globally, Act Locally

The well-known saying "think globally, act locally" is of utmost relevance to our efforts in raising the state of Islamic preaching in America at the local level. There are several things that every local community should do to help its pool of preachers become better preachers. Since many local communities are usually financially pressed, it is important to think of cost-efficient and practical approaches to meeting this objective, at least in the short term.

Once a module for a weekend preaching seminar has been developed, local communities should be invited to take advantage of it and host the seminar in their area. In the absence of such a professionally developed resource, local communities—with the support of recognized and experienced faith leaders—can put together their own workshop or reading group with the help of this guide. Just having the semblance of an organized gathering will bring preachers together to discuss and think about effective preaching. It is hoped that carefully reading through and discussing the ideas presented in this book will go some way to elevating the Friday prayer experience.

Local communities should also organize town hall–style conversations on various issues, in which preachers have an opportunity to interact with and especially *hear* from regular Friday prayer attendees. The topics of discussion should cover themes that can be addressed in a sermon. For example, a conversation could focus on the challenges of raising our youth. The point of this would be not for the preachers to offer another sermon on the topic but for them to carefully listen to the questions, concerns, and perspectives of people in the community. Preachers often suffer from a lack of awareness about the specific concerns of the congregations in which they preach or at least those of parts of their congregation. A preacher might be plugged into their own ethnic community within the congregation, for example, but lack awareness about issues that concern other ethnic communities within the same congregation. Hosting such conversations would help broaden the scope of understanding about relevant issues within the preaching community and greatly affect what and how preachers preach.

Along the same lines, going back to chapter 4, every community needs to develop an efficient and strong evaluation system in which the community is able to offer feedback and the preacher is able to benefit from such an assessment. It would be quite awkward and even demoralizing to distribute a *khuṭba* survey every week. Instead, evaluation forms can be made readily available online or on-site to be submitted anonymously at a congregant's convenience. Today, online surveys are easy to create and disseminate, but solely using this format risks excluding older community members or those without the privilege of internet access. The evaluations can then be compiled and further anonymized (if necessary) by an administrator in order to be shared with the respective *khaṭīb*. A wise and humble preacher will benefit enormously from such feedback.

It would also be of benefit for there to be greater coordination between *khaṭībs* and administrators so that topics for the *khuṭba* are chosen according to what is relevant and pressing in any given community. Another benefit of such coordination efforts is that the administration can develop an action-oriented initiative that can immediately put the message of a *khuṭba* into implementation to extend the preaching experience beyond the sermon. In effect, translate theory into practice. For example, if a *khaṭīb* preaches about *dhikr*, materials with prophetic and pious invocations can be made available after the worship service. It is a subtle and useful way of getting preachers to prepare well in advance and in concert with the needs and desires of their respective communities.

Even though finances are tight in many of our communities, for those communities with means, some degree of financial investment should be expected by their preachers. It might be as minor as granting scholarships to current or future preachers who want to develop their preaching skills. This might mean a grant to purchase relevant books, to attend useful classes, or to cover traveling costs for study and development. Time set aside for deeper growth is also important; periodic sabbaticals for a preacher should also be considered. Just as we invest in the repair, renovation, and expansion of our physical structures, so should we invest in the growth and betterment of our preachers. At the end of the day, even the most beautiful places of worship are illuminated with the beauty of Allah's teachings, which are conveyed through a wise preacher.

As such, a critical contribution that local communities can make to Islamic preaching in America is to offer reasonable compensation to preachers for their work so that they do not have to constantly worry about paying bills at home and can instead put that time and energy into developing the skills needed for great preaching. Simply put, we cannot expect to raise preaching standards without proper investment. And this must also include the creation of more well-paid positions for full-time Imams and scholars so that the field becomes a viable option for pious and intelligent Muslims who want to serve their community. Without a professionalization of the field of preaching, there is little chance of attracting the best youth to this important vocation. Physical structures are important, but what takes place inside of them is of greater magnitude. Truly worthy and long-lasting investments ought to be in our fellow human beings—in those who can inspire, teach, and guide hearts and minds to the service of Allah.

الله الله الله

Now let us conclude with the best of conclusions, with the remembrance of Allah the Guider of hearts, the Forgiver of sins, the Master of all affairs! In doing so, we read from Imam al-Ghazālī's final invocation in his advice to a beloved student-preacher:

> O God, I beg You in regard to grace for its completeness, in regard to protection for its permanence, in regard to mercy for its totality, in regard to wellbeing for its realization, in regard to livelihood for the most plentiful, in regard to life for the most happy, in regard to beneficence for the most perfect, in regard to favor for the most inclusive, in regard to generosity for the most sweet, and in regard to gentleness for the most intimate.
>
> O God, be for us and do not be against us! O God, conclude our lives with happiness, and make our hopes abundantly real, unite our mornings and evenings in wellbeing, and entrust our destiny and future state to Your mercy, pour the vessel of Your forgiveness over our sins, grant us the correction of our faults, make God-consciousness our provision, and make our exertion to be for Your religion, and our trust and our confidence to be in You.
>
> O God set us upon the path of righteousness, protect us in the world from causes of regret on the Day of Resurrection, lighten the weight of our sins, endow us with the way of life of the godly, restrain us from and avert from us the evil of the wicked, and release our necks and the necks of our fathers, mothers, brothers, and sisters from hellfire, by Your Mercy, You

Infinitely Precious, You Ever-Forgiving, You Bountiful One, You Veiler of sins, You Omniscient and Omnipotent!

O God, O God, O God! By Your Mercy, You Most Merciful of the Merciful, You First of all and Last of all, You Mighty Lord of Power, You who hast mercy on the needy, You Most Merciful of the Merciful, there is no god but You, glory be to You: I am a sinner! God bless our liege lord Muḥammad, all his Family and Companions, and praise belongs to God, the Lord of the Worlds.[1]

Afterword

by
Martin Nguyen

Even if the Day of Resurrection comes upon one of you while holding a seedling, plant it.

—*Aḥmad b. Ḥanbal,* Musnad al-imām Aḥmad b. Ḥanbal

For the Muslim who plants a tree or sows seeds and then a bird, person, or beast eats of it, that shall be a charity (*ṣadaqa*) for him.

—*Al-Bukhārī,* Ṣaḥīḥ al-imām al-Bukhārī

What We Leave Behind

One thousand four hundred and forty-two years after the Prophet Muhammad ﷺ established his nascent Muslim community in Medina, Sohaib Nazeer Sultan, the author of this work and my friend, passed away in his home in central New Jersey. He was forty years old. He left this life at the beginning of the holy month of Ramadan, one of the most sacred and treasured seasons in the Islamic accounting of time. His departure was accompanied by the setting of the sun, which, in that moment, marked our passage from the fourth day of Ramadan into its fifth. Sohaib departed, moreover, on the first Friday of Ramadan, *yawm al-jumu'a*, a blessed "day of gathering." When he breathed his last, he was far from alone. His friends and family were gathered by his side to see him on to the next life. Even at the end, Sohaib was able to bring together a rich array of souls.

I write these words many months after his passing, but I still vividly recall what happened afterward. In that raw span of time, his gift for gathering people together lived on. I witnessed it and was part of it—a community of faith in tumultuous motion pulled together by Sohaib's enduring presence. That so many of us were able to come together at all was a feat in and of itself given that uncertain period of time. Under normal circumstances, it is part of our religious tradition for the deceased to be laid to rest within a day's time. The circumstances at that time, however, were not normal. When Sohaib passed away on April 16, 2021, we had all been living with the difficulties of the Covid-19 pandemic for more than a year. Masking, social distancing, and bouts of isolation were all in place. Many traveled with trepidation or not at all. Large gatherings remained a risk. Within the Muslim community, congregational prayers were still far from reconvening with regularity. Vaccinations for adults were increasingly available but had not yet reached the degree of accessibility that they would enjoy by year's end. Vaccinations for children, however, were still many months away from approval. Sohaib's death transpired as things seemed to be taking a turn, though the turn had not quite arrived.

Like so many others, my family and I had spent the past year minimizing our travels while also limiting our circles of social engagement. Nevertheless, some trips, we felt, warranted the risks. There were some people who had to be seen. And so on March 6, we ventured down to see Sohaib one last time, though we were unsure at that time of that visit's finality. We had hoped to see him again, but his appointed time arrived beforehand. Thus on April 16, when news of Sohaib's death reached us in Connecticut, the question was not whether we should attend his funeral, but how best to do so. Despite the challenges raised by the pandemic, plans for a funeral had been readied and set. This was but one of the blessings that emerged from Sohaib's realization of his impending end. In the year between his terminal diagnosis and eventual demise, Sohaib had taken the time, especially in his final months, to think through and plan out the details of his last rites: the *janāza*, or "funeral" prayer, and his subsequent burial. He had a series of difficult discussions with his closest friends and loved ones in order to set his affairs in order so that when he did die, the community would not be left to spin adrift in this time of grief but know how to direct its mournful energies. Even in the face of death, Sohaib continued to think of all of those he would leave behind.

Connecting with our circle of friends in Connecticut, we decided to bring our families together in order to travel as a collective. While much happened that day, we were all able to arrive in time for the *janāza*. A public park had been selected for the service to provide an outdoor venue large enough to accommodate the larger crowds that were expected to arrive. As the field was slowly readied, the expected crowds arrived. They arrived in droves, hundreds upon hundreds of the faithful and faith-seeking. Over a long expanse of open grass, the faithful lined up in rows, standing distant from one another, masked, before a plot of earth where they could each stand and pray—apart but in unison. Although the dangers of the ongoing pandemic prevailed, incredibly many braved the situation out of deep respect, faith, and love, so that they might join Sohaib once more. Then when the *janāza* prayer was completed, that immense gathering wound its way from that grassy park field in a long caravan of cars to the cemetery some miles away in order to lay Sohaib to rest until the Day of Resurrection.

After such an extended time of isolation, the assembled throng of the faithful was breathtaking to behold. We had come from near and far. Members of local communities, those who had come to know Sohaib through his long service and work in the area, made up most of the multitude. Nonetheless, standing alongside them were many pockets of others, like ourselves, who had traversed greater distances to be there that day. From all across the Atlantic seaboard, friends and loved ones had come down from the far reaches of New England and up from North Carolina and Tennessee as well as places beyond. It was in the midst of this swell of people that so many paths were made to cross and reconnect again—a vibrant web of interconnections woven from out of Sohaib's life of faith. It was while traversing this web that I, to my surprise, was reunited with old friends and respected acquaintances long parted. Though we had all come for the sake of Sohaib, it was as if I was revisiting different periods of my own life as the day's events slowly unfolded. This too was part of Sohaib's legacy, that he had drawn so many of us into the orbit of his life such that we were also drawn closer to one another as well. I have taken the time to recount these events because all too often we shy from death and the wisdom it brings.

Many years before his own passing, Sohaib wrote poignantly about death in an essay titled "Living Life with Purpose." A beloved friend of his father, Ale Nabi, had died, and Sohaib went to visit his grave several weeks later to offer his prayers for him. Reflecting on this moment, he wrote,

> As I stood in prayer at Ale Nabi uncle's gravesite under the cold rain, what struck me the most was that his grave was completely unmarked—no name, no dates, no lasting words, nothing. Yet, the feeling of angelic presence around his grave was so powerful and overwhelming. It was a reminder that our true legacy as human beings is not found in what is inscribed on our tombstones when we die, but, rather, in the way that we live life and in the way we make a difference in the lives of people around us. The Prophet Muhammad taught us that when we die, the wealth and children we have amassed will not go with us in our graves nor will they be of any benefit to us. How true. Yet, too often we work so hard for wealth, status, glory and so much more, believing that our salvation and happiness lies in these accomplishments. But, the Prophet then added, "There are three things that continue to benefit you while you are in the grave: beneficial knowledge that you leave behind; the continuously beneficial acts of charity; and a child who prays for you." This prophetic teaching (*hadith*), sums up how we can live life with a purpose, a purpose that is greater than our own self and ego.[1]

When Sohaib's own end approached, it was no surprise, then, that he gave serious thought to what he might leave behind: beneficial knowledge, an ongoing form of charity, and a child who might pray for him.

Of these matters, this book encompasses two. The guidance that Sohaib offers here on the art and life of preaching represents, I believe, some of that knowledge that he leaves behind for us. At the same time, it was also envisioned by him as a form of charity. As he shared in a message to me a year before his death and at the start of our literary venture together, "I want to do this collaboration and would love to be able to leave something behind for the community on the topic of preaching as a *ṣadaqa jāriya*."[2] Indeed, this book expresses Sohaib's deep commitment to enriching the lives of faith of those who come after him and his desire to elevate the spiritual well-being of the Muslim community as a whole. Accept this book, then, as it was intended—as an ongoing gift. It is a gift to all those who Sohaib knew, a gift to all those he did not yet come to know, and a gift for all those yet to come.

With all that said, I would end, then, with the same lines that Sohaib used to conclude the reflective essay mentioned above:

> Life is not about what we achieve, but what we leave behind in the way of good for others. May we all find our life's purpose and live it out with sincerity and greatness. *Amīn.*[3]

Appendix

Du'ā's *from the Princeton Muslim Life Community*

COLLECTED IN THIS APPENDIX ARE *DU'Ā'S* or supplicatory prayers that were composed and delivered by women from the Princeton Muslim Life Community. We provide them here as a model and source of inspiration for others who might feel drawn to incorporate this practice into their personal or communal worship lives. The reasoning behind this practice and the experience of it within the author's community context is discussed at length in chapter 5.

Yusra Syed

Yusra was previously the assistant to the Muslim chaplain at Princeton University. She delivered the following du'ā' *at the end of the last in-person* jumu'a *held at Princeton before the university closed for the pandemic in 2020.*

I

O Allah, You are the Source of Mercy, the Giver of Mercy.

You are the All Powerful, the Healer, the Protector, the First and the Last.

We worship and we beseech none but You, as all things come from You alone.

And with that, as always, we ask You to send peace and blessings upon our beloved Prophet Muhammad and his family. We ask that You keep his light a source of illumination for our souls.

Allah . . . in such uncertain times, we ask for Your protection and Your guidance.

Allah, keep us conscious of You, let us continue to increase our worship, our reliance and trust in You and all Your affairs.

Let us upkeep our devotional practices on this blessed day of *jumu'a*.
Allow us to keep our faith and our communities.

Grant us, our communities, and our society a sense of ease in these circumstances. Let us remain calm and steadfast and think with reason.

Let us care for one another, help those in need. Keep us mindful to be present for those who need our help.

Allah, we ask that You protect us and our loved ones from this virus, protect our health, keep us from bodily harm if it is Your Will.

Protect our parents, our elders, the vulnerable, our brothers, our sisters, our children, our spouses, our beloveds, our friends.

Allah, we ask that You grant our students safe journeys home.
And for those remaining on campus, grant them Your protection,
grant their families Your protection, grant all ease during these times.

We plan and we plan, Allah . . . but what You have planned overcomes all.
For the lives that have been paused, disturbed, upended . . .
Grant us strength and patience and vision to see through these strange and uncertain times.

And may this be a reminder to be compassionate for those who are suffering throughout the world in dire circumstances.

For those who are and will be affected by this spread, we ask for Your relief and quick healing.

For those that are afflicted with health issues, whatever they may be, Allah, we ask that you grant them an easy healing, a means of expiation for their sins and strengthened faith in You.

Shower Your mercy upon all our caregivers, our practitioners, and our service workers.

Let us be a people and society that is able to handle and overcome this, let us be smart, let us be vigilant, let us be compassionate, let us be good humans.

We ask for relief for all people in anxiety over their education, homes, jobs, businesses . . . keep us afloat, keep us in a good state.

Allah, we are saddened by the circumstances for *jumu'a*. . . . Please keep our consciousness of You strong, let us engage in prayer, forgiveness, and continuous supplication.

Allah, allows us to see Ramadan, for it is about a month away. Lift up our souls and our hearts to prepare for it, see it, witness it, and end it with excellence.

We ask Allah, for all those suffering from trials in any form, of any gravity, that You alleviate their condition of difficulty, bring them towards ease, bring them out in stronger faith with a purified soul.

We pray, we pray, we pray for all those in harm's way throughout the cities, throughout the world.

You hold all power, You hold all wisdom. Our living and our dying is meant for You alone. We accept your trials, we accept your Will . . . just as we accept You as our One True Lord, and Your Prophet Muhammad as the seal of the messengers.

Only You hold the knowledge of when we will return to You.
Whether it
be today, in one month, or twenty years . . . the only thing we are sure of is that we will indeed return to You, our Creator, our Owner, our Master, our Lord.

Whenever our time may be, may we be on the best of terms with
You, in
the highest levels of consciousness and devotion to You—in which you accept us, forgive us, and allow us entrance into the eternal gardens of bliss in Your incredible, magnificent presence. We ask this for us and for all those we love.

With peace and blessings upon our beloved Prophet Muhammad,
we ask all
of this from You and more which we are unable to express through our words. You hear our words, You hear our hearts, You know our souls.

And we ask from none but You Allah, The Source of everything, The First and The Last, our Lord, our Creator.

Amīn

Sabrina Mirza

Sabrina holds a BA from Rutgers University in philosophy and Middle Eastern studies and a JD from Seton Hall University's School of Law. Her quest for religious studies led her to Vancouver, Canada, where she studied Qur'anic exegesis (tafsīr) *and spiritual excellence* (tazkiya) *under the renowned West African scholar Imam Fode Drame. Currently, she serves as the assistant to the Muslim chaplain and coordinator of the Muslim Life Program at Princeton University. She also practices law at a nonprofit in central New Jersey, where she represents unaccompanied minors seeking asylum and special immigrant juvenile status. The following* duʿā' *was delivered for a virtual* jumuʿa *gathering on September 4, 2020. The gathering marked the start of a new Islamic year, the beginning of the fall semester at Princeton University, and the ongoing Covid-19 pandemic.*

II

O Allah, O Most Merciful of those who show Mercy, all praise belongs to You.
Send prayers and peace upon our beloved messenger Muhammad, his family, and his companions.

Our Lord, in Your Name of Mercy, by Your Mercy, we begin . . .
We begin this academic year at Princeton and we begin this new Islamic year, earnestly seeking Your assistance.

O Opener of all doors, grant us an entrance of sincerity and an exit of sincerity.
Grant us Your openings of light and Your victories.
Grant us, most of all, closeness to You with each day, with each breath.
Find us continuously at Your door, seeking You who are too generous to turn us away, though You are All Seeing, All Aware of our transgressions.

O Forgiver of Sins, O Acceptor of Repentance, pardon us completely. Let us start anew with each beginning You bless us with, O Beginning of all Beginnings.

O Source of All Peace, O Reliever of Anxiety, where will we find peace in these uncertain times except in You?

O Granter of Safety, O Guardian of Faith, where will we find safety except in the fortress of our faith?

O Near One, O Answerer, O Fulfiller of Needs, relieve the troubles of the *umma* of Muhammad, upon him be peace. Unite those who are divided and answer the call of the oppressed.

O Protector, O You who watches over us with loving care, averting calamities from us that we are not even aware of, protect us and our loved ones from the Covid virus.

O You who sends down the cure with every disease, help us find a cure for our illnesses.

O source of all healing, heal our beloved teacher, Imam Sohaib, our dear sister Zoya Shoaib, and all those amongst us and our loved ones afflicted with illness. Grant them relief from their pain, ease in their hardship, and strengthen and elevate them through it, as well as their families.

O Allah, we ask for complete well-being for each of us, in our bodies, in our minds, and in our hearts.

Inspire us to delve deep within our hearts and help us navigate the darkness within—the traumas, the unmet needs, the diseases that may be festering. Send us guidance and true guides who bring us through the path safely with hearts that are sound and fully healed.
Bring our shortcomings to light gently so that we can see ourselves as we actually are, with compassion.

Help us break down the false image of ourselves that we project and connect us with our authentic selves; instill within us the courage and the commitment to persist in this labor of the heart, this journey to attaining our highest and truest potential.
For surely You made us in the most excellent form
and You love those who strive for excellence.

So let us strive with all of our being to reach Your close presence.
And we ask for Your grace because we cannot arrive without it.

O Most Generous and Most Merciful, open for us the doors of Your Mercy. Bless us to enter paradise with our loved ones, to dwell forever in the company of the righteous and the best of creation Muhammad, may perpetual prayers and peace be upon him, and upon his family and companions. *Amīn.*

Rachel Harrell-Bilici

Rachel Harrell-Bilici is a member of the Princeton Muslim community raising two Sunni-Shi'a, Kurdish American kids. She is a literary translator and editor of academic writing and serves as the academic coordinator for the Zahra Institute, a Chicago-based center for Kurdish studies. She composed and delivered the following three du'ā's *at the conclusion of several Friday prayer services held at Princeton.*

III

Ya Allah,
Today is the Winter Solstice, the shortest day of the year, the longest night of the year,
Today of all days, the order You establish in the cosmos stands plain before our eyes.

On this, the Shortest Day, we ask you:

Fill our brief days with work that is pleasing to you.
Help us feel the weight of our responsibility as your vice-regents on earth
and let us spend these hours caring for all of Your creation.
Send us hurrying after *ḥasanāt* like squirrels after nuts, so we have no time left for wickedness and folly.

On this, the Longest Night, we ask you:

Draw us close to You in prayer
and reassure us of Your listening presence.
Help us take an honest inward look, to assess our character and to amend it.
Make the long, still night the hour of our recommitment to You.

O You who cause daylight and darkness to ebb and flow around us,

In the brevity of winter days
teach us
to be diligent in Your service.

In the clarity of winter nights
teach us
the meaning of *yaqīn.*

Ṣallā Allāhu *ʿalā Muḥammad wa-ʿalā ahlihi al-ṭayyibīn al-ṭāhirīn.*

Amīn.

IV

The scorching month has come
Shower on us, Ya Allah, your cooling mercies.

The Qur'an is descending
Ya Allah, open our hearts to it.

The devils are chained
Our deeds, Ya Allah, are our own. Bend them all toward goodness.

We fast with our stomachs, our tongues, our eyes
Instill in us, Ya Allah, the habits of humility.

We seek the Laylat al-Qadr
Ya Allah, let our search be its own reward. Make our longing for forgiveness the means of our salvation.

We fast for You; we break our fast with Your sustenance; *al-ḥamdulillāh* stands on every tongue.

Accept it from us.

We turn our hearts to You by day, our prayers to You by night; the morning opens our eyes with *ṣubḥānallāh.*

Accept it from us.

We train our wills to submit to Your Will; make ourselves channels of Your Compassion, Your Beneficence, Your Light; every cell in our bodies reverberates *Allāhu akbār.*

Accept it from us.

Ya Allah, we ask You by Your signs
by the waxing moon,
by the lengthening days,
by the cool of evening and the sheltering night:

Accept from us our deeds in this Your month.

Ṣallā Allāhu ʿalā Muḥammad wa-ʿalā ahlihi al-ṭayyibīn al-ṭāhirīn.

Amīn.

V

Ya Allah, in these days we find ourselves bewildered by distance:
each street an unbridgeable gulf, another town as distant as the moon . . .
and, sealed up inside each house, a whole world teeming with activity.

O You who are closer to us than our jugular veins,
Unite us in spirit with our distant beloveds.
Guard them, nourish them, comfort them,
envelop them in Your care as we long to but cannot.

Sustaining Lord, who does not leave your creatures without provision,
Make us worthy companions to those who shelter with us.
Help us be sources of good counsel and good cheer,
Grant that we radiate calm in the face of anxiety
as Your constant, loving presence steadies and emboldens us.

In *Duʿāʾ Kumayl* we are taught to ask, "Ya Allah, be gracious to me in all my states . . ."
Even so, in distance and in nearness, in separation and confinement,

Teach us forbearance,
Assuage our fears,
Reward us with the reward of those who turn to You in calamity
and become reflectors of your *raḥma* to a wounded world.

Ṣallā Allāhu ʿalā Muḥammad wa-ʿalā ahlihi al-ṭayyibīn al-ṭāhirīn.

Amīn.

Arshe Ahmed

Arshe Ahmed is a community organizer and mother to Radiyya. Over the past ten years, she has been involved with helping organize Muslim communities at different universities. Arshe was the executive director (2014–18) for Medina Community Clinic, a nonprofit health organization, and now serves on the board of directors. She is on the organizing committee for the Mizaan Retreat, a family camp hosted by the Princeton University Muslim Life program. Arshe grew up in Brooklyn, New York, and currently lives in central New Jersey. The following duʿāʾ *was delivered on August 27, 2021, at the first in-person* jumuʿa *prayer service at Princeton University for the school's fall reopening.*

VI

Bismillāh wa'l-ḥamdulillāh wa'l-ṣalātu wa'l-salām ʿalā rasūl Allāh
In the name of Allah and Praise be to Allah, and May God's Peace and Blessings be upon the Messenger.

O Allah, we have been eagerly waiting for this *jumuʿa* day so make this gathering one full of blessings for each of us.
O Allah, remind us that *jumuʿa* is its own celebration. And a gathering of our souls, a gathering of our hearts.
O Allah, allow us, as believers, to reexperience the joy every single week for coming together to remember You in this space.
O Allah, we have gathered here for your presence. Grant us openings so that we can strive toward receiving Your presence.
O Allah, we ask You for the good of this day, its openings, lights, blessings, and right guidance.

O Allah, put us on the path of *istiqāma*—let us be steadfast in maintaining the good and virtue and all the lessons learned from this past year.

O Allah, we thank all of our teachers and mentors and sages who have showed us the way of guidance and beauty and right action in this life, especially in the last year. We ask You, ya Allah, to bless them with the highest of rewards and that you allow us to be people who follow in the path—the way of your beloved Prophet Muhammad. Peace and blessings be upon him.

O Allah, bless Sohaib who we remember most fondly and dearly.

Make us people of the Muhammadan way, not only in our outward actions but in our inner dimensions and in our hearts.

O Allah, make us people of *qalbun salīm*, a sound heart.
O Allah, surround us with angelic lights.

O Allah, give us the strength to ask for help.
O Allah, surround us with love and support when we need and allow us to be a means of love and support for others in need.

O Allah, allow us to realize these words: *Inna lillāhi wa-inna ilayhi raji'ūn.*
So that we understand that things are of a temporary nature, and to You is the return.
O Allah, grant us your LOVE in such a way that we long for You and for that day when we meet You.
O Allah, keep our tongues moist in Your remembrance, in *dhikr.*
O Allah, open our inner eyes to the signs around us and make us aware of Your Divine Presence.
May we gaze upon the luminosity of the sun and see the majesty of the light of God and let it penetrate toward our soul and heart.
May we gaze upon the ocean and realize the depths of the Qur'an through God's words.
O Allah, surround us with gentle rain that produces beautiful vegetation and a beautiful garden around us.

O Allah, make us amongst the *ṣābirūn* and grant us beautiful patience.
O Allah, make us amongst the *muttaqīn* and grant us God consciousness.
O Allah, make us amongst the *shākirūn* so we can be ever grateful.

O Allah, forgive us for our shortcomings and make us amongst the ones who forgive others.

O Allah, bless this gathering for you have poured your mercy and grace into this gathering.
We ask you, ya Allah, that you keep our hearts and souls united forever in this moment.

O Allah, we pray for everyone in humanity who are suffering and going through hardships.
O Allah, answer the distressed who call on You and relieve their suffering, and give them joy and comfort, both in this life and the hereafter.
O Allah, make us vehicles of bringing that joy and love and comfort into the world and for those people.

O Allah, grant us entrance into *Jannat al-firdaws*, a place of *salām*, a place of peace.
O Allah, we know our life in this world is a place of trial and tribulation and confusion and hardship but we know that You have promised us a life of total contentment and joy in the hereafter and so we are patient, ya Allah, for that entrance.
O Allah, make us of the people who are *raḍiya' Allāhu 'anhum wa-raḍū 'anhu*—those who You are content with and those who are content with You (Q. 98:8).

O Allah, send prayers, salutations, and blessings upon our Beloved Muhammad and increase us in our love for him, his Family, and his Companions!

O Allah, accept all of our *du'ā's* and prayers,
Amīn. Amīn. Amīn.

Notes

Foreword

1 Sohaib Sultan, *Searching for Wisdom: Ruminations on Islam Today—a Collection of Essays* (Princeton, NJ: Muslim Life Program in the Office of Religious Life, n.d.), 12.

2 Sohaib Sultan, telephone interview by Harvey Stark, June 16, 2014, transcript; Harvey Ronald Stark, "Looking for Leadership: Discovering American Islam in the Muslim Chaplaincy" (PhD diss., Princeton University, 2015), 143.

3 Stark, "Looking for Leadership," 154.

4 Sohaib Sultan, personal text message to Martin Nguyen, April 23, 2020.

5 Stark, "Looking for Leadership," 154.

6 Sultan, telephone interview by Stark.

7 Saʿd al-Dīn al-Taftazanī (d. 793/1390) engages with al-Nasafī's creed in his well-known commentary on it. Many other theologians held similar views with respect to the Qur'an as *kalām Allāh*. The tenth-century theologian al-Ṭaḥāwī (d. 321/933) writes something similar in his earlier creed: "The Qur'an is the Word of God that emanated from Him without modality in its expression. He sent it down to His messenger as a revelation. The believers accept it as such literally. They are certain it is, in reality, the Word of God, the Sublime and Exalted. Unlike human speech, it is eternal and uncreated." Saʿd al-Dīn al-Taftazānī, *A Commentary on the Creed of Islam: Saʿd al-Dīn al-Taftāzānī on the Creed of Najm al-Dīn al-Nasafī*, trans. Earl Edgar Elder (New York: Columbia University Press, 1950), 58; Al-Ṭaḥāwī, *The Creed of Imam al-Ṭaḥāwī: Al-Aqīdah al-Ṭaḥāwiyyah*, trans. Hamza Yusuf (Berkeley, CA: Zaytuna Institute, 2007), 54–55, articles 35–36.

8 The sermons of the Prophet ﷺ have been collected in numerous works. For example, see Abu Nasr Muhammad Ibn Wadʿan, *Sermons of the Prophet*

Muhammad, trans. Assad Nimer Busool (New Delhi: Goodword, 2002); and Mohammed Moinuddin Siddiqui, trans., *Sermons, Addresses and Discourses of the Messenger of Allah* (Chicago: Library of Islam, 2005).

9 Martin Lings, *Muhammad: His Life Based on the Earliest Sources* (Rochester, VT: Inner Traditions International, 1983), 334. Guillaume offers a similar translation that is based on Ibn Isḥāq's (d. 150/767) biography of the Prophet ﷺ: "O men, listen to my words. I do not know whether I shall ever meet you in this place again after this year." Ibn Isḥāq, *The Life of Muhammad: A Translation of Ibn Ishaq's Sirat Rasul Allah*, trans. A. Guillaume (Karachi, Pakistan: Oxford University Press, 2004), 651.

10 Sultan, telephone interview by Stark.

Introduction

1 Abū al-Faraj Ibn al-Jawzī, *Ibn al-Jawzī's Kitāb al-Quṣṣāṣ wa'l-Mudhakkirīn*, ed. and trans. Merlin L. Swartz (Beirut: Dar El-Machreq, 1986), 95.

2 Ibn al-Jawzī, 100–101.

3 Ibn al-Jawzī, 102.

4 Ibn al-Jawzī, 221.

5 Ibn al-Jawzī, 102.

6 Jonathan P. Berkey, *Popular Preaching and Religious Authority in the Medieval Islamic Near East* (Seattle: University of Washington Press, 2001); Konrad Hirschler, *The Written Word in the Medieval Arabic Lands: A Social and Cultural History of Reading Practices* (Edinburgh: Edinburgh University Press, 2012), 184–85. Among the religious scholars who penned critiques of the popular preachers were the Hanbalī scholar Ibn al-Jawzī, the Mālikī scholar Ibn al-Ḥājj al-ʿAbdarī (d. 737/1336), the Shāfiʿī scholar Zayn al-Dīn alʿIrāqī (d. 806/1403), the Andalusian jurist Muḥammad al-Ḥaffār (d. 842/1438), the Egyptian polymath al-Suyūtī (d. 911/1505), and the Moroccan sage Ibn Maymūn al-Idrīsī (d. 917/1511).

7 Berkey, *Popular Preaching*, 23.

8 Ibn al-Jawzī, *Kitāb al-Quṣṣāṣ wa'l-Mudhakkirīn*, 230. Also cited in Berkey, *Popular Preaching*, 24.

9 Hirschler, *Written Word*, 68. The quotation of al-Subkī is from al-Subkī, *Muʿīd al-niʿam wa-mubīd al-niqam*, ed. D. W. Myhrman (London: Luzac, 1908), 162–63.

10 Berkey notes that there was much tension between preachers and jurists for authority among the masses and wrangling over what interpretation of Islam the masses would follow. This analysis is confirmed by Ibn al-Jawzī, who dedicates an entire section of his book to condemn the harmful and

innovative practices that developed among the preachers. Berkey, *Popular Preaching*, 21.

11 Berkey, 24.

12 Nehemia Levtzion, "Patterns of Islamization in West Africa," in *Conversion to Islam*, ed. Nehemia Levtzion (New York: Holmes & Meier, 1979), 214.

13 Berkey, *Popular Preaching*, 39.

14 In the Christian tradition, the art of preaching is known as homiletics.

15 Ibn al-Jawzī, *Kitāb al-Quṣṣāṣ wa'l-Mudhakkirīn*, 96.

16 Ibn al-Jawzī, 97.

17 Berkey, *Popular Preaching*, 65.

18 Berkey, 12.

19 Wael Alkhairo, *Speaking for Change: A Guide to Making Effective Friday Sermons* (Beltsville, MD: Amana, 1428/1998), 1.

20 Ibn al-Jawzī, *Kitāb al-Quṣṣāṣ wa'l-Mudhakkirīn*, 68–70.

21 Mazen Hashem, *The Muslim Friday Khutba: Veiled and Unveiled Themes* (Clinton Township, MI: Institute for Social Policy and Understanding, October 2009), https://www.ispu.org/the-muslim-friday-khutba-veiled-and-unveiled-themes/.

22 Thomas Cleary, *The Wisdom of the Prophet: The Sayings of Muhammad* (Boston: Shambhala, 2001), 1.

Chapter I: On the Purposes of Preaching

1 A "master story" is an account or set of accounts that binds a group of people together around a common narrative. For instance, the story of the Prophet ﷺ first receiving Qur'anic revelation makes for a Muslim "master story." Ronald J. Allen, "The Social Function of Language in Preaching," in *Preaching as a Social Act: Theology and Practice*, ed. Arthur Van Seters (Nashville: Abingdon, 1988), 167.

2 Hashem, *Muslim Friday Khutba*, 11.

3 Ibn Wad'an, *Sermons of the Prophet Muhammad*, 59–60 (translation modified by Sultan).

4 Abū Ḥāmid al-Ghazālī, *Letter to a Disciple: Ayyuhā'l-Walad*, trans. Tobias Mayer (Cambridge: Islamic Texts Society, 2005), 48–51.

5 Ibn al-Jawzī, *Kitāb al-Quṣṣāṣ wa'l-Mudhakkirīn*, 106.

6 Ibn al-Jawzī, 107.

7 Ibn al-Jawzī, 231.

8 Ibn al-Jawzī, 230.

9 Abū al-Ḥusayn Muslim b. al-Ḥajjāj al-Qushayrī al-Naysābūrī, *Ṣaḥīḥ Muslim*, ed. Muḥammad Fu'ād 'Abd al-Bāqī, 5 vols. (Cairo: Dār Iḥyā' Kutub al-'Arabiyya, 1955–56), 4:2060, chap. 47 *kitāb al-'ilm*, no. 16, p. 2674. Also cited in Ibn al-Jawzī, *Kitāb al-Quṣṣāṣ wa'l-Mudhakkirīn*, 230.

10 Siddiqui, trans., *Sermons, Addresses and Discourses*, 48–49 (translation modified by Sultan).

11 Al-Ghazālī, *Letter to a Disciple*, 50–53 (emphasis added).

12 Ibn al-Jawzī, *Kitāb al-Quṣṣāṣ wa'l-Mudhakkirīn*, 230.

13 Berkey, *Popular Preaching*, 33 (emphasis added).

14 Alkhairo, *Speaking for Change*, 2, 6.

15 Abū Zakariyyā Yaḥyā b. Sharaf al-Nawawī al-Dimashqī, *Commentary on the Riyâd-us-Sâliheen (Sharḥ riyādh al-ṣāliḥīn)*, vol. 1, commentary by Salahuddin Yusuf, trans. Muhammad Amin and Abu Usamah Al-Arabi bin Razduq (Riyadh, Saudi Arabia: Darussalam, 1999), 189–90, hadith 181 (translation by Sultan).

16 Al-Nawawī, 191, hadith 183 (translation by Sultan).

17 Al-Nawawī, 241, hadith 245.

18 Al-Nawawī, 192–93, hadiths 184, 199, 194 (translation by Sultan). See also Sohaib Sultan, *The Koran for Dummies* (Hoboken, NJ: Wiley, 2004), 208, 239.

19 Siddiqui, *Sermons, Addresses and Discourses*, 85 (translation modified by Sultan).

20 Alkhairo, *Speaking for Change*, 1.

Chapter 2: On the Life and Character of a Preacher

1 Al-Nawawī, *Riyâd-us-Sâliheen*, 204–5, hadith 198.

2 Ibn al-Jawzī, *Kitāb al-Quṣṣāṣ wa'l-Mudhakkirīn*, 208.

3 Arthur Stephen Hoyt, *The Preacher: His Person, Message, and Method* (New York: Macmillan, 1909), 3.

4 Ibn al-Jawzī, *Kitāb al-Quṣṣāṣ wa'l-Mudhakkirīn*, 109–10.

5 Ibn al-Jawzī, 111 (translation by Sultan and Nguyen).

6 Al-Nawawī, *Riyâd-us-Sâliheen*, 19, hadith 7.

7 Al-Ghazālī, *Letter to a Disciple*, 40–41.

8 Abū Ḥāmid al-Ghazālī, *The Beginning of Guidance*, 2nd ed., rev. and ed. Abdur-Rahman ibn Yusuf Mangera, trans. Mashhad al-Allaf (White Thread, 2010); Hamza Yusuf and Zaid Shakir, *Agenda to Change Our Condition* (Sandala, 2013); William C. Chittick, *Science of the Cosmos, Science of the Soul: The Pertinence of Islamic Cosmology in the Modern World* (Oxford: Oneworld, 2007); Ahmed Paul Keeler, *Rethinking Islam and the West* (Cambridge: Equilibra, 2019).

9 Mālik b. Anas, *al-Muwaṭṭā'*, ed. Muḥammad ʿAbd al-Raḥmān al-Marʿashlī (Beirut: Dār Iḥyā al-Turāth al-ʿArabī, 1424/2003), 556, book 47 *kitāb ḥusn al-khalq*, report 694; Mālik b. Anas, *Al-Muwatta of Imam Malik ibn Anas: The First Formulation of Islamic Law*, trans. Aisha Abdurrahman Bewley (Inverness, UK: Madinah, 2004), 382, book 47 "Good Character," hadith 8.

10 Al-Nawawī, *Riyâd-us-Sâliheen*, 74, hadith 54 (translation modified by Sultan).

11 Al-Bukhārī, *Ṣaḥīḥ al-imām al-Bukhārī al-musammā al-jāmiʿ al-musnad al-ṣaḥīḥ al-mukhtaṣar min umūr rasūl Allāh wa-sunanihi wa-ayyāmihi*, ed. Muḥammad Zuhayr b. Nāṣir al-Nāṣir, 9 vols. (Beirut: Dār Ṭawq al-Najāh, 2002), 1:33, book 3 *kitāb al-ʿilm*, chap. 38, hadith 107. See also hadiths 106, 108.

12 This line was spoken by Dr. King in his speech "Beyond Vietnam: A Time to Break the Silence," which was delivered on April 4, 1967, at Riverside Church in New York City. In that speech, Dr. King repeats and reflects upon this line, which was issued initially by the organization known as Clergy and Laymen Concerned about Vietnam. Martin Luther King Jr., *A Call to Conscience: The Landmark Speeches of Dr. Martin Luther King, Jr.*, ed. Clayborne Carson and Kris Shepard (New York: Warner, 2001), 140.

13 The line was delivered by Dr. King in Georgia at the Albany Mass Movement meeting at Shiloh Baptist Church on August 15, 1962. Variations of this line appear in several of Dr. King's speeches as well. Martin Luther King Jr., *The Papers of Martin Luther King, Jr.*, vol. 7, *To Save the Soul of America, January 1961–August 1962*, ed. Clayborne Carson and Tenisha Armstrong (Berkeley: University of California Press, 2014), 593. See also Martin Luther King Jr., "Remaining Awake through a Great Revolution," in *A Knock at Midnight: Inspiration from the Great Sermons of Martin Luther King, Jr.* (New York: IPM/Warner, 1998), 204–24; and Martin Luther King Jr., "Some Things We Must Do," in *The Papers of Martin Luther King, Jr.*, vol. 4, *Symbol of the Movement, January 1957–December 1958*, ed. Clayborne Carson et al. (Berkeley: University of California Press, 2000), 328–43, esp. 331.

14 Hoyt, *Preacher*, 16–17.

15 Abū Ḥāmid al-Ghazālī, *The Ninety-Nine Beautiful Names of God*, trans. David Burrell and Nazih Daher (Cambridge: Islamic Texts Society, 1997), 117.

16 Umar Faruq Abd-Allah, "Mercy: The Stamp of Creation," Nawawi Foundation, 2004, p. 2, https://www.theoasisinitiative.org/nawawi-mercy.

17 Hoyt, *Preacher*, 16.

18 Al-Ghazālī, *Ninety-Nine Beautiful Names*, 54.

19 Muslim, *Ṣaḥīḥ Muslim*, 1:93.

20 Ibn al-Jawzī, *Kitāb al-Quṣṣāṣ wa'l-Mudhakkirīn*, 123 (translation modified by Sultan).

21 Al-Nawawī, *Riyâd-us-Sâliheen*, 581, hadith 682 (translation by Sultan).

22 Ibn al-Jawzī, *Kitāb al-Quṣṣāṣ wa'l-Mudhakkirīn*, 112–13.
23 Ibn al-Jawzī, 174.
24 Abū ʿAbd Allāh Muḥammad b. Yazīd al-Qazwīnī Ibn Majāh, *Sunan Ibn Majāh*, ed. Bashshār ʿAwwād Maʿrūf, 6 vols. (Beirut: Dār al-Jīl, 1418/1998), 1:214–15, *al-muqaddima*, hadith 224.
25 Hashem, *Muslim Friday Khutba*, 14.
26 Gibrīl Fouād Ḥaddād, *The Four Imams and Their Schools: Abū Ḥanīfa, Mālik, al-Shāfiʿī, Aḥmad* (London: Muslim Academic Trust, 2007), 176; Ibn ʿAbd al-Barr, *al-Intiqāʾ fī faḍāʾil al-aʾimma al-thalātha al-fuqahāʾ: Mālik wa'l-Shāfiʿī wa-Abī Ḥanīfa*, ed. ʿAbd al-Fattāḥ Abū Ghudda (Beirut: Dār al-Bashāʾir al-Islāmiyya, 1997), 75.
27 *lā adrī nifs al-ʿilm*. Abū Bakr al-Bayhaqī, *al-Madkhal fī'l-sunan al-kubrā*, ed. Muḥammad Ḍiyāʾ al-Raḥmān al-Aʿẓamī (Ṣabāḥiyya, Kuwait: Dār al-Khulafāʾ li-Kitāb al-Salāmī, n.d.), 435, hadith 810.
28 Sherman Jackson, *Islam and the Problem of Black Suffering* (Oxford: Oxford University Press, 2009).
29 Malcolm X and Alex Haley, *The Autobiography of Malcolm X* (New York: Grove, 1965), 173.
30 Hoyt, *Preacher*, 31.
31 Hoyt, 160.
32 Ibn al-Jawzī, *Kitāb al-Quṣṣāṣ wa'l-Mudhakkirīn*, 219.
33 Al-Ghazālī, *Letter to a Disciple*, 56–57.
34 Al-Nawawī, *Riyâd-us-Sâliheen*, 234, hadith 236.
35 Al-Bukhārī, *Ṣaḥīḥ al-imām*, 7:31, book 67 *kitāb al-nikāḥ*, chap. 89, *hadith* 5199.
36 Hoyt, *Preacher*, 51.
37 Al-Nawawī, *Riyâd-us-Sâliheen*, 458, hadith 516 (translation by Sultan).
38 Hoyt, *Preacher*, 58.
39 Al-Ghazālī, *Beginning of Guidance*, 60–61.
40 Hoyt, *Preacher*, 36.
41 Hoyt, 25.

Chapter 3: On the Craft of Sermon Writing

1 Allah Most High says in *sūrat al-raʿd*, *Are not hearts at peace in the remembrance of God?* (Q. 13:28).
2 Hoyt, *Preacher*, 50.
3 Muslim, *Ṣaḥīḥ Muslim*, 130–31, *kitāb al-īmān*, hadith 232, reports 145–46; Aḥmad b. Ḥanbal, *Musnad al-imām Aḥmad b. Ḥanbal*, ed. Shuʿayb al-Arnaʾūṭ et al., 50 vols. (Beirut: Muʾassasat al-Risāla, 1995–2001), 6:325, report 3784;

Aḥmad b. Ḥanbal, *Musnad*, 11:230–31, report 6650; Ibn Majah, *Sunan Ibn Majāh*, 5:468–69; Abū ʿĪsā Muḥammad b. ʿĪsā al-Tirmidhī, *al-Jāmiʿ al-kabīr*, ed. Bashshār ʿAwwād Maʿrūf, vol. 4 (Beirut: Dār al-Gharb al-Islāmī, 1996), 371–73, *abwāb al-īmān*, section 13, hadiths 2629–30.

4 Hoyt, *Preacher*, 84.

5 Al-Bukhārī, *Ṣaḥīḥ al-imām*, 4:34, book 56 *kitāb al-jihād*, chap. 70, hadith 2886; Ibn Majāh, *Sunan Ibn Majāh*, 5:574, book 37 *kitāb al-zuhd*, hadiths 4135–36.

6 Roger J. Allen, ed., *Patterns of Preaching: A Sermon Sampler* (St. Louis, MO: Chalice, 1998), x–xii.

7 Webb Garrison, *The Preacher and His Audience* (Fleming Revell, 1954), 64.

8 Allen, *Patterns of Preaching*, xi–xii.

9 Allen, 7–8.

10 Allen, 22–23.

11 Allen, 29–30.

12 Allen, 36–37.

13 Originally called "Bipolar Preaching," this form has been renamed "Contrasting Perspectives." Allen, 49–50.

14 Allen, 64–65.

15 Allen, 64.

16 Allen, 93–94.

17 Allen, 93.

18 Lowry is quoted in Allen, 93–94.

19 Allen, 94.

20 Allen, 149–50.

21 Garrison, *Preacher and His Audience*, 109.

22 Garrison, 109.

23 Garrison, 110.

24 Garrison, 110.

25 William A. Graham, *Divine Word and Prophetic Word in Early Islam* (The Hague, Netherlands: Mouton, 1977), 127, saying 12; Ibrahim Kunna, ed., *110 Ahadith Qudsi: Sayings of the Prophet Having Allâhs Statements*, trans. Syed Masood-ul-Hasan (Riyadh, Saudi Arabia: Darussalam, 2006), 11, hadith 1.

26 Garrison, *Preacher and His Audience*, 111.

27 Garrison, 111.

28 Garrison, 111.

29 Garrison, 112.

30 Garrison, 112.

31 Garrison, 113.

32 Garrison, 100.

33 Garrison, 228.

34 Garrison, 183.
35 Garrison, 189.
36 Garrison, 178.
37 Garrison, 185.
38 Garrison, 186–89.
39 Ibn al-Jawzī, *Kitāb al-Quṣṣāṣ wa'l-Mudhakkirīn*, 127.
40 Al-Nawawī, *Riyâd-us-Sâliheen*, 595, hadith 700 (translation by Sultan).
41 Ibn al-Jawzī, *Kitāb al-Quṣṣāṣ wa'l-Mudhakkirīn*, 229.
42 Ibn al-Jawzī, 229.
43 Ibn al-Jawzī, 197.
44 Ibn al-Jawzī, 198.
45 Al-Nawawī, *Riyâd-us-Sâliheen*, 549, hadith 637.
46 Garrison, *Preacher and His Audience*, 66.
47 Garrison, 77.

Chapter 4: On the Delivery of the Sermon

1 Ibn al-Jawzī, *Kitāb al-Quṣṣāṣ wa'l-Mudhakkirīn*, 113.
2 Al-Nawawī, *Riyâd-us-Sâliheen*, 667, hadith 803 (translation by Sultan).
3 Al-Nawawī, 658, hadith 790.
4 Alkhairo, *Speaking for Change*, 31.
5 The verse is specifically repeated thirty-one times in *sūrat al-Raḥmān*, chap. 55. The verses are as follows: 13, 16, 18, 21, 23, 25, 28, 30, 32, 34, 36, 38, 40, 42, 45, 47, 49, 51, 53, 55, 57, 59, 61, 63, 65, 67, 69, 71, 73, 75, 77.
6 Garrison, *Preacher and His Audience*, 80.
7 Garrison, 93.
8 Garrison, 239.
9 Al-Bukhārī, *Ṣaḥīḥ al-imām*, 7:53, book 68 *kitāb al-ṭalāq*, hadith 5304.
10 Al-Bukhārī, 3:129, book 46 *kitāb al-maẓālim*, hadith 2446.
11 Garrison, *Preacher and His Audience*, 78.
12 Garrison, 65.
13 Garrison, 87.
14 Berkey, *Popular Preaching*, 28–29.
15 Hoyt, *Preacher*, 368.
16 Ibn al-Jawzī, *Kitāb al-Quṣṣāṣ wa'l-Mudhakkirīn*, 207.

Chapter 5: On Women and the Friday Prayer Service

1 Ingrid Mattson, "Can a Woman Be an Imam? Debating Form and Function in Muslim Women's Leadership," https://ingridmattson.org/article/can-a-woman-be-an-imam/; Ingrid Mattson, "Can a Woman Be an Imam? Debating Form and Function in Muslim Women's Leadership," in *The Columbia Sourcebook of Muslims in the United States*, ed. Edward Curtis IV (New York: Columbia University Press, 2008), 253.

2 Abū Zakariyyā Yaḥyā b. Sharaf al-Nawawī al-Dimashqī, *An-Nawawī's Forty Hadith: An Anthology of the Sayings of the Prophet Muhammad*, trans. Ezzeddin Ibrahim and Denys Johnson-Davies (Cambridge: Islamic Texts Society, 1997), 34–35, hadith 3, see also pp. 28–29, hadith 2 (translation by Sultan).

3 Abū Dāwūd al-Sijistānī, *Sunan Abu Dawud*, trans. Ahmad Hasan, vol. 1 (New Delhi: Kitab Bhavan, 2003), 150, *kitāb al-ṣalāt*, hadiths 569–70. See also Abū al-Ḥusayn Muslim b. al-Ḥajjāj al-Qushayrī al-Naysābūrī, *Ṣaḥīḥ Muslim: Being Traditions of the Sayings and Doings of the Prophet Muḥammad as Narrated by His Companions and Compiled under the Title al-Jāmi'-uṣ-Ṣaḥīḥ*, trans. 'Abdul Ḥamīd Ṣiddīqī, 4 vols. (n.p.: n.d.) 1:241, *kitāb al-ṣalāt*, hadith 895.

4 In addition to this report from Sāḥīḥ Muslim (hadith 886), see the many others in collections like Muslim, *Ṣaḥīḥ Muslim: Being Traditions*, 1:240–41, *kitāb al-ṣalāt*, hadiths 884–91; and Abū Dāwūd, *Sunan Abu Dawud*, 149, *kitāb al-ṣalāt*, hadiths 565–68.

5 Hammer has critically studied the 2005 woman-led Friday prayer service as well as its larger implications for American Muslim discourses on women, gendered prayer spaces, and religious authority. Chapters 1 and 2 discuss the prayer event and the debates surrounding it, while chapter 6 examines broader questions of women's leadership within mosque spaces. Juliane Hammer, *American Muslim Women, Religious Authority, and Activism: More Than a Prayer* (Austin: University of Texas Press, 2012), 13–55, 124–46.

6 Asma Sayeed, *Women and the Transmission of Religious Knowledge in Islam* (New York: Cambridge University Press, 2013). On a related note, Mohammad Akram Nadwi has prepared in English an introductory work based on a forty-volume biographical dictionary of women hadith transmitters in Arabic. Mohammad Akram Nadwi, *al-Muḥaddithāt: The Women Scholars in Islam* (Oxford: Interface, 2007).

7 Aisha Geissinger, *Gender and Muslim Constructions of Exegetical Authority: A Rereading of the Classical Genre of Qur'ān Commentary* (Leiden: Brill, 2015).

8 Marion Holmes Katz, *Women in the Mosque: A History of Legal Thought and Social Practice* (New York: Columbia University Press, 2014), 111–98.

9 Sayeed, *Women and the Transmission*, 118.

10 Sayeed, 115–18.

11 Sayeed, 115–18.

12 Jonathan A. C. Brown, *Misquoting Muhammad: The Challenge and Choices of Interpreting the Prophet's Legacy* (London: Oneworld, 2004), 199. Katz also documents this example. Katz, *Women in the Mosque*, 152.

13 Mirjam Künkler, "Women as Religious Authorities: What a Forgotten History Means for the Modern Middle East," Rice University's Baker Institute for Public Policy, October 2, 2018, p. 2, https://www.bakerinstitute.org/sites/default/files/2018-10/import/bi-brief-100218-cme-carnegie-kunkler.pdf.

14 Katz, *Women in the Mosque*, 195.

15 Saba Mahmood, *Politics of Piety: The Islamic Revival and the Feminist Subject* (Princeton, NJ: Princeton University Press, 2005); Pieternella van Doorn-Harder, *Women Shaping Islam: Reading the Qur'an in Indonesia* (Urbana: University of Illinois Press, 2006); Feryal Salem, "The Emergence of Women's Scholarship in Damascus during the Late 20th Century," in *The Routledge Handbook of Islam and Gender*, ed. Justine Howe (London: Routledge, 2020), 318–27; Maria Jaschok and Shui Jingjun Shui, *The History of Women's Mosques in Chinese Islam: A Mosque of Their Own* (Richmond, UK: Curzon, 2000).

16 While a wide variety of published pieces are available, see especially Brown's *Misquoting Muhammad* and the aforementioned work by Hammer, *American Muslim Women*. As Brown demonstrates, the opposition to women-led prayer is built more on a deep adherence to tradition rather than clear, authenticated proof texts from either the Qur'an or hadith. Brown, *Misquoting Muhammad*, 189–99; Hammer, *American Muslim Women*, 36–55.

17 Sultan, telephone interview by Stark.

Conclusion

1 Al-Ghazālī, *Letter to a Disciple*, 60 (translation modified by Sultan and Nguyen).

Afterword

1 Sohaib Sultan, "Living Life with Purpose," in *Searching for Wisdom*, 23. The essay was originally published online as Sohaib Sultan, "An Islamic Reflection on Living Life with Purpose," *HuffPost*, contributor blog, March 13, 2012, https://www.huffpost.com/entry/living-life-with-a-purpose_b_1203141.

2 Sultan, personal text message to Nguyen. I have italicized and retransliterated the phrase *sadaqa jariyya* that appeared originally in the text.

3 Modified by Nguyen. Sultan, "Living Life with Purpose," 24.

Bibliography

Abd-Allah, Umar Faruq. "Mercy: The Stamp of Creation." Nawawi Foundation, 2004, https://www.theoasisinitiative.org/nawawi-mercy.

Abdul-Matin, Ibrahim. *Green Deen: What Islam Teaches about Protecting the Planet.* San Francisco: Berrett-Koehler, 2010.

Abū Dāwūd al-Sijistānī. *Sunan Abu Dawud.* Translated by Ahmad Hasan. 3 vols. New Delhi: Kitab Bhavan, 2003.

Abugideiri, Salma, and Mohamed Hag Magid. *Before You Tie the Knot: A Guide for Couples.* Self-published, CreateSpace, 2014.

Ahmed, Sameera, and Mona M. Amer, eds. *Counseling Muslims: Handbook of Mental Health Issues and Interventions.* New York: Routledge, 2012.

Akram Nadwi, Mohammad. *al-Muḥaddithāt: The Women Scholars in Islam.* Oxford: Interface, 2007.

Alkhairo, Wael. *Speaking for Change: A Guide to Making Effective Friday Sermons.* Beltsville, MD: Amana, 1428/1998.

Allen, Ronald J., ed. *Patterns of Preaching: A Sermon Sampler.* St. Louis, MO: Chalice, 1998.

———. "The Social Function of Language in Preaching." In *Preaching as a Social Act: Theology and Practice,* edited by Arthur Van Seters, 167–204. Nashville: Abingdon, 1988.

al-Bayhaqī, Abū Bakr. *al-Madkhal fī'l-sunan al-kubrā.* Edited by Muḥammad Ḍiyā' al-Raḥmān al-A'ẓamī. Ṣabāḥiyya, Kuwait: Dār al-Khulafā' li-Kitāb al-Salāmī, n.d.

Berkey, Jonathan P. *The Formation of Islam: Religion and Society in the Near East, 600–1800.* Cambridge: Cambridge University Press, 2003.

———. *Popular Preaching and Religious Authority in the Medieval Islamic Near East.* Seattle: University of Washington Press, 2001.

Brown, Jonathan A. C. *Misquoting Muhammad: The Challenge and Choices of Interpreting the Prophet's Legacy.* London: Oneworld, 2004.

al-Bukhārī. *Ṣaḥīḥ al-imām al-Bukhārī al-musammā al-jāmiʿ al-musnad al-ṣaḥīḥ al-mukhtaṣar min umūr rasūl Allāh wa-sunanihi wa-ayyāmihi.* Edited by Muḥammad Zuhayr b. Nāṣir al-Nāṣir. 9 vols. Beirut: Dār Ṭawq al-Najāh, 2002.

Chan-Malik, Sylvia. *Being Muslim: A Cultural History of Women of Color in American Islam.* New York: New York University Press, 2018.

Chittick, William C. *Science of the Cosmos, Science of the Soul: The Pertinence of Islamic Cosmology in the Modern World.* Oxford: Oneworld, 2007.

Cleary, Thomas. *The Wisdom of the Prophet: The Sayings of Muhammad.* Boston: Shambhala, 2001.

Curtis, Edward E., IV. *Muslims in America: A Short History.* Oxford: Oxford University Press, 2009.

Er, Muhammad Emin. *Laws of the Heart: An Introduction to the Spiritual Path in Islam.* Translated by Joseph Walsh. Atlanta: Shifa, 2008.

Garrison, Webb. *The Preacher and His Audience.* Fleming Revell, 1954.

Gawande, Atul. *Being Mortal: Medicine and What Matters in the End.* New York: Metropolitan, 2014.

Geissinger, Aisha. *Gender and Muslim Constructions of Exegetical Authority: A Rereading of the Classical Genre of Qurʾān Commentary.* Leiden: Brill, 2015.

al-Ghazālī, Abū Ḥāmid. *The Beginning of Guidance,* 2nd ed. Revised and edited by Abdur-Rahman ibn Yusuf Mangera, translated by Mashhad al-Allaf. White Thread, 2010.

———. *Letter to a Disciple: Ayyuhā'l-Walad.* Translated by Tobias Mayer. Cambridge: Islamic Texts Society, 2005.

———. *The Ninety-Nine Beautiful Names of God.* Translated by David Burrell and Nazih Daher. Cambridge: Islamic Texts Society, 1997.

Graham, William A. *Divine Word and Prophetic Word in Early Islam.* The Hague, Netherlands: Mouton, 1977.

Ḥaddād, Gibrīl Fouād. *The Four Imams and Their Schools: Abū Ḥanīfa, Mālik, al-Shāfiʿī, Aḥmad.* London: Muslim Academic Trust, 2007.

Hammer, Juliane. *American Muslim Women, Religious Authority, and Activism: More Than a Prayer.* Austin: University of Texas Press, 2012.

———. *Peaceful Families: American Muslim Efforts against Domestic Violence.* Princeton, NJ: Princeton University Press, 2019.

Hashem, Mazen. *The Muslim Friday Khutba: Veiled and Unveiled Themes.* Clinton Township, MI: Institute for Social Policy and Understanding, October 2009. https://www.ispu.org/the-muslim-friday-khutba-veiled-and-unveiled-themes/.

Helwa, A. *Secrets of Divine Love: A Spiritual Journey into the Heart of Islam.* Capistrano Beach, CA: Naulit, 2020.

Hirschler, Konrad. *The Written Word in the Medieval Arabic Lands: A Social and Cultural History of Reading Practices.* Edinburgh: Edinburgh University Press, 2012.

Hoyt, Arthur Stephen. *The Preacher: His Person, Message, and Method.* New York: Macmillan, 1909.

Ibn ʿAbd al-Barr. *al-Intiqāʾ fī faḍāʾil al-aʾimma al-thalātha al-fuqahāʾ: Mālik waʾl-Shāfiʿī wa-Abī Ḥanīfa.* Edited by ʿAbd al-Fattāḥ Abū Ghudda. Beirut: Dār al-Bashāʾir al-Islāmiyya, 1997.

Ibn Ḥanbal, Aḥmad. *Musnad al-imām Aḥmad b. Ḥanbal.* Edited by Shuʿayb al-Arnaʾūṭ et al. 50 vols. Beirut: Muʾassasat al-Risāla, 1995–2001.

Ibn Isḥāq. *The Life of Muhammad: A Translation of Ibn Ishaq's Sirat Rasul Allah.* Translated by A. Guillaume. Karachi, Pakistan: Oxford University Press, 2004.

Ibn al-Jawzī, Abū al-Faraj. *Ibn al-Jawzī's Kitāb al-Quṣṣāṣ waʾl-Mudhakkirīn.* Edited and translated by Merlin L. Swartz. Beirut: Dar El-Machreq, 1986.

Ibn Majāh, Abū ʿAbd Allāh Muḥammad b. Yazīd al-Qazwīnī. *Sunan Ibn Majāh.* Edited by Bashshār ʿAwwād Maʿrūf. 6 vols. Beirut: Dār al-Jīl, 1418/1998.

Ibn Naqib al-Misri, Ahmad. *Reliance of the Traveller: A Classical Manual of Islamic Sacred Law,* rev. ed. Translated by Nuh Ha Mim Keller. Beltsville, MD: Amana, 1994.

Ibn Wadʿan, Abu Nasr Muhammad. *Sermons of the Prophet Muhammad.* Translated by Assad Nimer Busool. New Delhi: Goodword, 2002.

Jackson, Sherman. *Islam and the Problem of Black Suffering.* Oxford: Oxford University Press, 2009.

Jaschok, Maria, and Shui Jingjun Shui. *The History of Women's Mosques in Chinese Islam: A Mosque of Their Own.* Richmond, UK: Curzon, 2000.

Kamali, Mohammed Hashim. *Shari'ah Law: An Introduction.* Oxford: Oneworld, 2008.

Katz, Marion Holmes. *Women in the Mosque: A History of Legal Thought and Social Practice.* New York: Columbia University Press, 2014.

Keeler, Ahmed Paul. *Rethinking Islam and the West.* Cambridge: Equilibra, 2019.

King, Martin Luther, Jr. *A Call to Conscience: The Landmark Speeches of Dr. Martin Luther King, Jr.* Edited by Clayborne Carson and Kris Shepard. New York: Warner, 2001.

———. *A Knock at Midnight: Inspiration from the Great Sermons of Martin Luther King, Jr.* New York: IPM/Warner, 1998.

———. *The Papers of Martin Luther King, Jr.* Vol. 4, *Symbol of the Movement, January 1957–December 1958.* Edited by Clayborne Carson, Susan Carson, Adrienne Clay, Virginia Shadron, and Kieran Taylor. Berkeley: University of California Press, 2000.

———. *The Papers of Martin Luther King, Jr.* Vol. 7, *To Save the Soul of America, January 1961–August 1962.* Edited by Clayborne Carson and Tenisha Armstrong. Berkeley: University of California Press, 2014.

Künkler, Mirjam. "Women as Religious Authorities: What a Forgotten History Means for the Modern Middle East." Rice University's Baker Institute for Public Policy, October 2, 2018, p. 2. https://www.bakerinstitute.org/sites/default/files/2018-10/import/bi-brief-100218-cme-carnegie-kunkler.pdf.

Kunna, Ibrahim ed. *110 Ahadith Qudsi: Sayings of the Prophet Having Allâhs Statements.* Translated by Syed Masood-ul-Hasan. Riyadh, Saudi Arabia: Darussalam, 2006.

Levtzion, Nehemia. "Patterns of Islamization in West Africa." In *Conversion to Islam,* edited by Nehemia Levtzion, 207–216. New York: Holmes & Meier, 1979.

Lings, Martin. *Muhammad: His Life Based on the Earliest Sources.* Rochester, VT: Inner Traditions International, 1983.

Mahmood, Saba. *Politics of Piety: The Islamic Revival and the Feminist Subject.* Princeton, NJ: Princeton University Press, 2005.

Mālik b. Anas. *Al-Muwaṭṭā'.* Edited by Muḥammad 'Abd al-Raḥmān al-Mar'ashlī. Beirut: Dār Iḥyā al-Turāth al-'Arabī, 1424/2003.

———. *Al-Muwatta of Imam Malik ibn Anas: The First Formulation of Islamic Law.* Translated by Aisha Abdurrahman Bewley. Inverness, UK: Madinah, 2004.

Mattson, Ingrid. "Can a Woman Be an Imam? Debating Form and Function in Muslim Women's Leadership." In *The Columbia Sourcebook of Muslims in the United States,* edited by Edward Curtis IV, 252–263. New York: Columbia University Press, 2008.

———. *The Story of the Qur'an: Its History and Place in Muslim Life.* Malden, MA: Blackwell, 2008.

Mogahed, Yasmin. *Reclaim Your Heart: Personal Insights on Breaking Free from Life's Shackles.* San Clemente, CA: FB Publishing, 2012.

Mohiuddin, Meraj. *Revelation: The Story of Muhammad, Peace and Blessings Be upon Him.* Scottsdale, AZ: Whiteboard, 2016.

Morgan, Michael Hamilton. *Lost History: The Enduring Legacy of Muslim Scientists, Thinkers, and Artists.* Washington, DC: National Geographic, 2007.

Murata, Sachiko, and William C. Chittick. *The Vision of Islam.* St. Paul, MN: Paragon House, 1994.

Muslim b. al-Ḥajjāj al-Qushayrī al-Naysābūrī, Abū al-Ḥusayn. *Ṣaḥīḥ Muslim.* Edited by Muḥammad Fu'ād 'Abd al-Bāqī. 5 vols. Cairo: Dār Iḥyā' Kutub al-'Arabiyya, 1955–1956.

———. *Ṣaḥīḥ Muslim: Being Traditions of the Sayings and Doings of the Prophet Muḥammad as Narrated by His Companions and Compiled under the Title al-Jāmi'-uṣ-Ṣaḥīḥ.* Translated by 'Abdul Ḥamīd Ṣiddīqī. 4 vols. n.p.: n.d.

Nabahani, Yusuf. *Muhammad: His Character and Beauty—Wasa'il al-Wusul ila Shama'il al-Rasul.* Translated by Abdul Aziz Suraqah. Al-Madina Institute, 2015.

al-Nawawī. *An-Nawawī's Forty Hadith: An Anthology of the Sayings of the Prophet Muhammad.* Translated by Ezzeddin Ibrahim and Denys Johnson-Davies. Cambridge: Islamic Texts Society, 1997.

al-Nawawī al-Dimashqī, Abū Zakariyyā Yaḥyā b. Sharaf. *Commentary on the Riyâd-us-Sâliheen (Sharḥ riyādh al-ṣāliḥīn).* Commentary by Salahuddin Yusuf, translated by Muhammad Amin and Abu Usamah Al-Arabi bin Razduq. 2 vols. Riyadh: Darussalam, 1999.

Nguyen, Martin. *Modern Muslim Theology: Engaging God and the World with Faith and Imagination*. Lanham, MD: Rowman & Littlefield, 2019.

Palfrey, John, and Urs Gasser. *Born Digital: How Children Grow Up in a Digital Age*. Rev. and expanded ed. New York: Basic Books, 2016.

Renard, John. *Islam and Christianity: Theological Themes in Comparative Perspective*. Berkeley: University of California Press, 2011.

Salem, Feryal. "The Emergence of Women's Scholarship in Damascus during the Late 20th Century." In *The Routledge Handbook of Islam and Gender*, edited by Justine Howe, 318–327. London: Routledge, 2020.

Sayeed, Asma. *Women and the Transmission of Religious Knowledge in Islam*. New York: Cambridge University Press, 2013.

Siddiqui, Mohammed Moinuddin, trans. *Sermons, Addresses and Discourses of the Messenger of Allah*. Chicago: Library of Islam, 2005.

Smith, Mikaeel Ahmed. *With the Heart in Mind: The Moral and Emotional Intelligence of the Prophet (S)*. Qasim, 2019.

Stark, Harvey Ronald. "Looking for Leadership: Discovering American Islam in the Muslim Chaplaincy." PhD diss., Princeton University, 2015.

al-Subkī. *Muʿīd al-niʿam wa-mubīd al-niqam*. Edited by D. W. Myhrman. London: Luzac, 1908.

Sultan, Sohaib. *The Koran for Dummies*. Hoboken, NJ: Wiley, 2004.

———. *The Qur'an and Sayings of the Prophet Muhammad: Selections Annotated and Explained*. Woodstock, VT: SkyLight Illuminations, 2007.

———. *Searching for Wisdom: Ruminations on Islam Today—a Collection of Essays*. Princeton, NJ: Muslim Life Program in the Office of Religious Life, n.d.

al-Taftazānī, Saʿd al-Dīn. *A Commentary on the Creed of Islam: Saʿd al-Dīn al-Taftāzānī on the Creed of Najm al-Dīn al-Nasafī*. Translated by Earl Edgar Elder. New York: Columbia University Press, 1950.

al-Ṭaḥāwī. *The Creed of Imam al-Ṭaḥāwī: al-Aqīdah al-Ṭaḥāwiyyah*. Translated by Hamza Yusuf. Berkeley, CA: Zaytuna Institute, 2007.

Tatum, Beverly Daniel. *Why Are All the Black Kids Sitting Together in the Cafeteria? and Other Conversations about Race*. 20th anniversary ed. New York: Basic Books, 2017.

al-Tirmidhī, Abū ʿĪsā Muḥammad b. ʿĪsā. *al-Jāmiʿ al-kabīr*. Edited by Bashshār ʿAwwād Maʿrūf. 6 vols. Beirut: Dār al-Gharb al-Islāmī, 1996.

van Doorn-Harder, Pieternella. *Women Shaping Islam: Reading the Qur'an in Indonesia*. Urbana: University of Illinois Press, 2006.

X, Malcolm. *Malcolm X Speaks: Selected Speeches and Statements*. Edited by George Breitman. New York: Grove, 1965.

X, Malcolm, and Alex Haley. *The Autobiography of Malcolm X*. New York: Grove, 1965.

Yusuf, Hamza, and Zaid Shakir. *Agenda to Change Our Condition*. Sandala, 2013.

Qur'anic Verse Index

General Index